CHILD APPRENTICES IN AMERICA

From Christ's Hospital, London
1617-1778

Child Apprentices in America

from Christ's Hospital, London
1617-1778

Peter Wilson Coldham

GENEALOGICAL PUBLISHING CO., INC.

Introduction

The prominent part played by Christ's Hospital scholars in the formation of colonial America in the fields of government, mercantile affairs, estate management and shipping, pose an obvious question. Why, until now, have the excellent registers of this ancient institution escaped the attention of the many researchers seeking to discover and make public the English roots of early emigrants? All the records of Christ's Hospital have, after all, been freely available in the London Guildhall for the last fifteen years. Perhaps one reason is that the only part of the registers so far published has been the first volume covering the years 1554 to 1599.[1] Clearly the precise role which the alumni were to be allotted in succeeding years was not to be foreseen in the pages of this publication, though the signs were already there that many would be selected for influential posts in England's rapidly developing empire. Another deterrent to making selective abstracts from the registers is the sheer amount of work that is entailed. In the eight volumes of registers examined covering the years 1605-1775 there are probably more than 30,000 separate entries. Fewer than one student in every twenty, therefore, was destined to figure in American history.

Brief History of the Hospital

By the second half of the sixteenth century the dramatic increase in the number of London poor, disabled and orphaned required urgent action, and the City fathers devised a scheme which would provide, according to the lights of that time, a remedy for these social ills. A contemporary assessment identified three principal classes of inhabitants who were to be the beneficiaries:

Introduction

1. Those made poor or homeless by no fault of their own, such as fatherless children, the "decayed" and the crippled.

2. Those impoverished by disease or accident.

3. Those reduced to want by their own idleness or vice.

The orphaned in the first category, provided they were legitimate children of freemen of the City of London, would be educated and given a good start in life in a new foundation to be known as Christ's Hospital; those in the second group would be cared for in St. Thomas's Hospital; and those in the third division taken into an institution, the Bridewell, where they could be restrained, corrected, and put to useful work.

Christ's Hospital was founded in 1553 on the site of an ancient monastery in Newgate Street known as Greyfriars and, in its first year, 400 children were taken in. The original articles of the foundation required that each child presented for admission should be provided with a baptismal certificate from his native parish and a signed declaration that he/she was not born outside lawful wedlock. With infrequent exceptions, admission was restricted to sons and daughters of freemen of the City Companies who were over four years of age and free from obvious infirmity. Furthermore, only one child of the same father could be housed in the Hospital at the same time. Gradually the residential and patrimonial restrictions were relaxed, although the age qualification appears to have been raised so that by 1674 no child under the age of seven was resident.

As the seventeenth century drew to a close the number of students being educated in Newgate Street (and in Ware, Hertford and Hoddesdon where the Hospital maintained schools) had risen to 1,000, and from then until the early 1800s up to 150 children were admitted each year on the recommendation of their parishes, and a further ninety or so under the terms of charitable endowments. Each academic year began at Easter and all vacant spaces were filled at that time, those awaiting placement being slotted in during the ensuing months as vacancies were created by deaths, discharges or withdrawals.

Both the City of London and its alumni were fiercely proud of the *Bluecoat School*, so named because of the blue cloak which, together with a special badge, distinguished the students. An offence certain to bring instant dismissal was to show disrespect for the uniform, and more than one lad escaped the disciplinary rigours of the school by selling his cloak or throwing his badge on a dunghill. Despite, or perhaps because of, the harsh discipline, Christ's Hospital achieved an academic standard which was unrivalled in London, and those few with sufficient intelligence, fortitude and application were able to graduate to one of the Oxford or Cambridge colleges; even the less able could look forward to a valuable apprenticeship. The roll of past students includes such celebrities as Charles Lamb, Samuel Taylor Coleridge and James Henry Leigh Hunt.

From its foundation the Hospital was not without personal ties to the New World. The first alumnus to be noted in the Americas was Thomas Sexton, whose career in Virginia was cut short by the Indian massacre at Jamestown in 1622. Next in line was Elias Corlett, who went up to Lincoln College, Oxford, in 1626 and became the master of a grammar school in New England supplying scholars to the newly-established Harvard College. Another old Christ's scholar, Ezechiel Cheever, studied at Emanuel College, Oxford, before going in 1637 to Boston, where he taught for over seventy years. One Gabriel Jones should also be noticed here. He was born on a farm near Williamsburg, Virginia, in 1724 and taken to London by his mother to be admitted to Christ's Hospital in 1732. Seven years later he was apprenticed to a lawyer before returning to Virginia and rising to the office of King's Attorney for Frederick County in 1743 at the age of nineteen. His fame and fortune increased after his marriage in 1749 and, having acquired a large estate in Augusta County and found a friend in George Washington, he died at the age of eighty-two in 1806[2].

7

Notes on the Records Used

The records of Christ's Hospital, many complete from the time of its foundation, well written, well preserved and integrally indexed, are housed in the Manuscript Department of the London Guildhall (Aldermanbury, London EC2P 2EJ). Those of greatest value to the genealogical researcher are:

Children's Registers (MS 12,818). *See below.*

Presentation Papers from 1674 (MS 12,818A). These are files of correspondence relating to the admission of *some* of the children into the Hospital.

Registers of Discharges and Apprenticeships from 1673 (MS 12,876). These record the same information, sometimes with additional detail, as is found in the Children's Registers but omitting dates of birth and admission.

Acquittance Books from 1647 to 1749 (MS 12,825). These contain "receipts" for the scholars upon their leaving the Hospital.

The principal source for the compilation of this book, augmented by occasional reference to the Registers of Discharges, has been the Children's Registers. These were kept as "double-entry" ledgers. As soon as a child was admitted an entry was made on the left-hand page recording the name of the new scholar, his date of birth or baptism, native parish and any other salient information, together with the name and occupation of the father. The right-hand page was completed as soon as the child came off the roll because of death, expulsion, removal by a parent, desertion, apprenticeship or advancement to a university. Except where bindings were to captains of ships, a boy or girl taking up an apprenticeship had to receive the written consent of his/her next-of-kin whose signature often appears in the ledger together with the signature of the master or his agent.

Arrangement of Entries

Each entry is presented in the same chronological order as in the original Registers but in an abbreviated form. In particular, it has not been thought necessary to include the phrase "citizen of London" beside fathers' names because the inclusion of a trade will normally imply such citizenship. Similarly, the word "deceased," where it occurs in the original as qualifying the father, has been omitted. In those few instances where a father remained alive, the fact will appear in the discharge entry.

The spelling of personal names has exactly followed the original, but other matter, including geographical locations, has been rendered into modern English; and all dates have been interpreted according to the modern calendar.

The division of the original Registers is by years, each starting in March or April, and this plan has been followed in the book from 1674 onwards. After the start of each academic year a few additional children were often admitted to fill vacated places, but frequently without a note of the date of their admission. Such later additions can usually be identified by the qualifying phrase "in the place of."

Acknowledgment

My thanks are due to the staff of the Manuscript Department of the Guildhall Library for their advice and assistance during the preparation of this work.

Peter Wilson Coldham   AMDG
Purley, Surrey, England   Michaelmas 1989

---

[1] See a pamphlet of 1918 by A.M. Lockhart entitled *Gabriel Jones, sometime scholar of Christ's Hospital, an American citizen.*

[2] See *Christ's Hospital Admissions,* Vol. 1, published by Harrison of London, 1937.

Edward Searles aged 3, son of Gregory S., bricklayer, admitted from St. Sepulchre 5 April 1606; 18 August 1618 to the Virginia Company.

Humphrey Kent aged 5, son of John K., merchant tailor, admitted from St. Sepulchre 18 March 1607; 17 October 1617 sent to his mother in Virginia.

Richard Marrett aged 4, son of Richard M., butcher, admitted 25 April 1607; 2 May 1619 to Mr. Richard Chamberlaine for the Somer Islands.

John Martine aged 4, son of Thomas M., haberdasher, admitted from St. Sepulchre 16 March 1608; 20 May 1619 to Mr. Richard Chamberlaine for the Somer Islands.

Thomas Heath aged 4, son of Jeremy H., whitebaker, admitted from St. Giles Cripplegate 23 March 1608; 2 May 1619 put to Lady Altome and sent to Virginia in September 1621.

Aziell Ely aged 4, son of William E., skinner, admitted at the request of the Commissioners for Virginia 5 October 1609; 9 October 1617 to be sent to his parents in Bermuda.

John Hill aged 4, half son of Otewell H., cordwainer, admitted from St. Brides's 2 April 1610; 18 August 1617 apprenticed to the Virginia Company.

John Prince aged 8, son of John P., leatherseller, admitted from St. Andrew Wardrobe 20 March 1613; 20 May 1619 to Richard Chamberlaine to be sent to the Somer Islands. [Mary Prince, daughter of same, discharged 2 June 1620].

Robert Okey aged 12, son of Francis O., waterman, admitted at the request of the Recorder of London 7 June 1615; 12 August 1619 to the Virginia Company.

Mary Bland aged 2, daughter of Jerome B., vintner, admitted from St. Sepulchre 9 April 1616; May 1621 sent to Bermuda with her mother, Mary Frith.

George Frith aged 3, son of George F., goldsmith, admitted from St. Foster's 24 April 1623; 1 July 1633 sent to the Somer Islands by discretion of Alderman Parkhurst.

John Byne aged 5 admitted at the request of the Treasurer 25 January 1657; September 1667 apprenticed to Mr. John Newton, merchant, to be sent to Barbados.

John Civell aged 8, son of Thomas Civell, admitted from Hackney 28 April 1657; September 1659 sent to Bermuda by his said father.

James Becknall, born 2 June 1663, son of James B., citizen of London, admitted from St. Botolph Aldgate 22 February 1670; October 1677 to be sent to Col. Newton in Barbados to serve him.

Thomas Vicars, born 1 May 1661, son of Thomas V., feltmaker, admitted from St. Olave Southwark 7 March 1670; October 1675 to the grandfather, William French, living in New Rents, Southwark, to be sent to his father Mr. Thomas Vicars, now a Minister living in Petson Parish, Gloucester Co., Virginia.

Abraham Dumbleton, born 8 May 1662, son of Abraham D., baker, admitted from St. Stephen Coleman Street 7 March 1670; 8 August 1677 to James Kendall, commander of the *Clara* bound for Jamaica.

Thomas Price, born 19 September 1662, son of Rowland P., clothworker, admitted from St. Dunstan in the East 2 April 1670; December 1673 to Robert Smith, commander of the *Mary* bound for Barbados.

James Applin, born 15 March 1662, son of Joseph A., draper, admitted from St. Botolph Aldgate 27 February 1671; 9 August 1677 to Robert Morris, commander of the *Young Prince* bound for Virginia.

Joseph Wells, born 7 November 1662, son of Richard W., carman, admitted from St. Andrew Wardrobe 27 February 1671; September 1677 to John Munford, citizen and grocer, to serve in Virginia.

Savell Wright, born 2 February 1663, son of Savell W., merchant, admitted from St. Sepulchre 27 February 1671; April 1679 to Capt. John —, commander of the *Hope* bound for Barbados.

Edward Sheldon, born 24 January 1666, son of Edward S., leatherseller, admitted from St. Giles Cripplegate 2 March 1671; March 1682 to Andrew Cratey Jr., commander of the *Bonadventure* bound for New England.

Joseph Terry, born 10 February 1662, son of John T., lorriner, admitted from St. Michael Bassishaw 8 March 1671. 28 July 1677 to Matthew Yates, commander of the *Recovery* bound for Jamaica.

John Peckover alias Pettifer, born Finsbury baptised 20 January 1667, son of John P., weaver, admitted from St. Giles Cripplegate 8 January 1673; September 1682 to Joseph Bartholomew, commander of the *Providence* bound for Jamaica.

Edward Flood, born 13 Jan. 1661, son of John Flood, leatherseller, admitted from St. Giles Cripplegate in November 1673; 12 September 1677 to Joseph Wilde, commander of the *Prince* bound for Jamaica.

Thomas Chamberlaine, born 2 Feb. 1661, son of William Chamberlaine, citizen and baker deceased, admitted from All Hallows Barking November 1673; 28 May 1677 to James Kendall, commander of the *Clara* bound for Jamaica.

Admissions in April 1674

Edward Richards, born 3 April 1664, son of Samuel Richards, haberdasher, admitted from St. Dunstan in the East; April 1679 to David Lockwood, commander of the *Dragon* bound for Jamaica.

Henry Cordwell, born 25 December 1664, son of William C., grocer, admitted from Norton in the City of Hertford; September 1679 to Nathan Reynolds, commander of the

Sarratt Merchant bound for Virginia.

John West, born 22 September 1665, son of Richard W., plasterer, admitted from from St. Katherine Creechurch; March 1681 to James Manby, commander of the *Arabella* bound for Barbados.

Deliverance Cotterell, born 26 March 1665, son of Richard C., dyer, admitted from St. Leonard Shoreditch; August 1679 to John Consett, commander of the *Mary* bound for Virginia.

John Sturmey, born 12 January 1667, son of Edmond S., grocer, admitted from St. Dunstan in the West; 13 February 1680 to John Jewell, commander of the *Batchelor* bound for Barbados.

Samuell Burgis, born 25 March 1667, son of Nicholas B., merchant tailor, admitted from St. Katherine Creechurch; February 1681 to Christopher Ravens, commander of the *Loyal Goring* bound for Barbados.

Richard Hart, son of George H., tallow chandler, admitted from St. Dunstan in the East; 11 July 1681 to Joseph Graves, commander of the *Bohemia Merchant* bound for Barbados.

Charles Sherbourne, born 14 March 1665, son of Charles S., barber surgeon, admitted from St. Giles Cripplegate; 1680 to Samuel Jones, commander of the *Joanna* bound for Jamaica.

Admissions in April 1675

Benjamin Watson, born 29 September 1666, son of William W., clothworker, admitted from St. Giles Cripplegate; 6 June 1683 to Peter Paggen, commander of the *Booth* bound for Virginia.

John Howman, born 3 March 1667, son of John H., admitted from St. Mary Somerset; 1680 to Richard Cobb, commander of the *Resolution* bound for Barbados.

Isaac Ward, born 29 March 1669, son of Richard W., clothworker, admitted from St. Giles Cripplegate; July 1680 to Robert Conaway, commander of the *Prince* bound for Virginia.

Richard Hodgskins, born 26 January 1666, son of Richard H., blacksmith, admitted from St. Botolph Aldgate; February 1680 to Peter Blake, commander of the *Elizabeth* bound for Jamaica.

Jacob Ward, born 9 December 1670, son of Richard W., clothworker, admitted from St. Botolph Bishopsgate; 22 May 1686 to Leonard Browne, commander of the *Anne* bound for Angola and Jamaica.

Admissions in April 1677

Thomas Trippett [or Triplett], aged 3, son of William T., blacksmith, admitted from St. Bride's; 11 July 1685 to Benjamin Hall, commander of the *William & Mary* bound for Virginia.

Richard Crockett, born 31 January 1667, son of Thomas C., stationer, admitted from St. Benet Paul's Wharf; 22 May 1683 to Thomas Hazelwood, commander of the *Katherine* bound for Virginia.

Nathaniel Long, born 8 October 1668, son of Thomas L., merchant tailor, admitted from St. Giles Cripplegate; 22 May 1683 to Bartholomew Clement, commander of the *Rose & Crown* bound for Virginia.

Charles Laughorne, born 12 November 1666, son of Richard L., admitted from St. Bride's; 22 May 1683 to William Jefferys, commander of the *Concord* bound for Virginia.

Admissions in April 1678

John Davis, born 24 July 1669, son of John D., blacksmith, admitted from St. Dunstan in the West; 4 March 1686 to John Benson, commander of the *Scipio* bound for Barbados.

John Alday, son of William A., merchant tailor, admitted from St. James Clerkenwell; 2 August 1681 to John Mumford, citizen and grocer, to serve in Virginia.

Richard Wilkinson [or Wilkington], born 17 March 1667, son of Richard W., bricklayer, admitted from Holy Trinity; 9 April 1684 to James Leech, commander of the *John & Elizabeth* bound for Barbados.

William Wise, born 2 March 1670, son of Thomas W., haberdasher, admitted from from St. Olave Southwark; 21 November 1685 to Arthur Smith, commander of the *Amity* bound for the West Indies.

Abell Barnard, born 17 July 1668, son of Joell B., skinner, admitted from St. Martin in the Fields; 25 August 1685 to Thomas Gardner, commander of the *Fortune* bound for Virginia.

Anthony Payne, born 20 July 1669, son of Anthony P., baker, admitted from St. Andrew Holborn; 23 May 1685 to Thomas Aubone, commander of the *Hopewell* bound for Barbados.

Bennet Smith, born 8 June 1668, son of Bennet S., needle maker, admitted from St. Botolph Aldgate; 26 September 1682 to his said father and to Captain Benjamin King, commander of the *Biscay Merchant* bound for Barbados.

Admissions in April 1679

James Vaughan, born 1 September 1672, son of Roger V., leatherseller, admitted from St. Sepulchre; 23 September 1687 to Mr. Henry Hartwell of James Town, Virginia, merchant.

John Sadler, born 16 December 1670, son of Robert S., haberdasher, admitted from St. Mary at Hill; 27 July 1689 to John Williams, commander of the *Richard & Michael* bound for Barbados.

William Davis, born 16 September 1671, son of Nicholas D., blacksmith, admitted from St. Michael Queenhithe;

4 December 1685 to Nathaniel Bacon of Virginia, merchant.

John Browne, born 27 April 1671, son of Isaac B., apothecary, admitted from Stepney; 22 May 1686 to Christopher Keeble, commander of the *Vealz Merchant* bound for New England.

Anthony Eales, born 15 October 1670, son of Thomas E., haberdasher, admitted from St. Botolph Aldgate; 29 August 1688 to Benjamin King, commander of the *Constant Richard* bound for Barbados.

Edmond Edon, born 15 August 1672, son of John E., skinner, admitted from St. Christopher's; 31 May 1690 to Richard Whiffing, commander of the *Port Royal Merchant* bound for Jamaica.

Admissions in April 1680

Joseph Wallis, born 23 February 1673, son of Edward W., dyer, admitted from St. Olave Southwark; 31 May 1690 to John Soane, commander of the *Jeffrey* bound for Guinea and the West Indies.

Ezekiel Muller, born 16 April 1671, son of Peter M., haberdasher, admitted from Stepney; 9 January 1689 to Robert Lurting, commander of the *Young Prince* bound for Virginia.

John White, born 10 June 1670, son of Samuel W., barber surgeon, admitted from St. Pancras Soper Lane; 9 October 1686 to Thomas Warren, commander of the *Society* bound for Barbados.

Francis Booth, born 7 May 1673, son of Francis B., haberdasher, admitted from St. Dunstan in the West; 12 February 1690 to William Covell, commander of the *William & Mary* bound for the West Indies.

Admissions in April 1681

Richard Francklin, born 18 August 1673, son of Henry F., salter, admitted from St. Stephen Coleman Street; 26 June 1688 to Mrs. Margaret Farewell living in Basinghall Street to be bound to her son George Farewell, an attorney in Boston, New England.

John Hooke, born 15 April 1674, son of John H., barber surgeon, admitted from All Hallows Bread Street; 21 August 1689 to Michael Staples, commander of the *Edward & Mary* bound for the West Indies.

John French, born 20 November 1672, son of Robert F., admitted from St. Pancras, Middlesex; 12 February 1690 to Peregrine Browne, commander of the *Anne* bound for Virginia.

Admissions in April 1682

John Sherrington, born 15 September 1673, son of Joshua S., merchant tailor, admitted from St. Michael Bassishaw; 21 August 1689 to James Smith, commander of the *Sedgwick* bound for Barbados and Jamaica.

Edmond Gethings, born 15 November 1675, son of Richard G., clothworker, admitted from St. Katherine Coleman; November 1689 to Robert Morton, barber surgeon living in Wapping, bound to Jamaica as surgeon of one of H.M. ships.

Francis Claxton, born 13 July 1673, son of Richard C., "musicianer," admitted from St. Michael Bassishaw; 4 April 1688 to Mr. William Wrayford, merchant in Bow Lane, be sent to Nicholas Tippett and Mary his wife in St. Christopher's.

Henry Conway, born 15 November 1673, son of John C., clothworker, admitted from St. Martin Orgar; 20 April 1689 to Leonard Edgcomb, commander of the frigate *Royal Hudson Bay* bound to Hudson's Bay.

Edward Athy, born 28 March 1675, son of Edward A., cooper, admitted from St. George Botolph Lane; 28 December 1689 to Col. Philip Ludwell of Virginia by the consent of his brother John Athy, cooper.

William Rowland, born 11 October 1674, son of William R., merchant tailor, admitted from St. Olave Southwark; 5 October 1692 to Robert Curtis, commander of the *Seven Brothers* bound for Barbados.

Nathan Gase, born 10 November 1673, son of John G., saddler, admitted from St. Peter Cornhill; 29 October 1690 to Elihu Robinson, commander of the *Francis & Samuell* bound for Virginia.

Samuell Edwards, born 28 July 1672, son of Thomas E., mariner, admitted from St. Olave Hart Street; 27 July 1689 to Stephen Carket, commander of the *Charity* bound for the West Indies.

Edward Wilton, born 29 September 1673, son of Mathew W., admitted from St. Sepulchre; 11 October 1690 to Matthew Ryder, commander of the *Caecilia* bound for Virginia.

Admissions in April 1683

Thomas Nash, born 24 March 1676, son of Walter N., dyer, admitted from St. Martin Vintry; 10 October 1691 to his mother Rebecca Creed to serve Richard Bate of Fauston, Derbys, Esq. and to go with him to Barbados.

John Swetnam, baptised 29 November 1674, son of Thomas S., clothworker, admitted from St. Andrew Holborn; 4 May 1692 to William Jeffreys, commander of the *Sarah* bound for Virginia.

Thomas Panck, baptised 10 March 1675, son of Jeremy P., butcher, admitted from St. Botolph Aldgate; 14 October 1691 to John Smith, commander of the *Diamond* bound for Jamaica.

William Robinson, born 10 March 1674, son of William R., painter stainer, admitted from St. Giles Cripplegate; 23 March 1688 to his uncle Richard Robinson and aunt Mary Curtis to serve William Stretton, commander of the *Golden Lyon* bound for Barbados with the agreement of his mother Mary R.

George Quintine, born 12 April 1676, son of William Q., weaver, admitted from St. Leonard Shoreditch; 19 December 1689 to his uncle Henry Quintine and to Micajah Perry and Thomas Lane of St. Katherine Creechurch, merchants, to serve William Cole Esq. in Virginia.

Admissions in April 1684

Peter Jenks, born 29 September 1676, son of Christopher J., grocer, admitted from St. Clement Danes; 7 November 1693 to Michael Staples, commander of the *Edward & Mary* bound for the West Indies.

Paul Payne, born 2 January 1672, son of John P., apothecary, admitted from All Hallows on the Wall; 26 January 1689 to Thomas Burrell, commander of the *Turkey Merchant* bound for the West Indies.

Thomas Pickering, born 23 August 1674, son of Francis P., merchant tailor, admitted from St. Saviour Southwark; 4 May 1692 to John Corbett, commander of the *Beaver* bound for New York.

John Newsam, baptised 11 November 1672, son of John N., goldsmith, admitted from Stepney; 2 November 1687 to George Richards of St. Botolph Aldgate, merchant, to be assigned to Col. John Page of York River, Virginia.

Thomas Rogers, baptised 6 December 1675, son of Roger R., admitted from St. Nicholas, Rochester, Kent; 27 April 1689 to John Brome, commander of the *Ruth* bound for Barbados.

William Vaile, born 8 January 1674, son of William V., painter, admitted from Lambeth, Surrey; 11 October 1690 to Thomas Willey, commander of the *Laurel* bound for the West Indies.

Thomas Tranter, born 2 March 1673, son of Thomas T., clothworker, admitted from St. Mary le Savoy; 10 May 1690 to Samuell Isaac, commander of the *Virginia Factor* bound for Virginia.

Benjamin Wallington, born 15 May 1674, son of William W., fishmonger, admitted from St. Nicholas Cole Abbey; 14 October 1691 to Joseph Old, commander of the *Good Success* bound for the West Indies.

Jeffrey Atkinson, born 9 November 1674, son of Stephen A., admitted from St. Anne Blackfriars; 7 May 1691 to Christopher Prissie, commander of the *Bridgetown* bound for Barbados.

William Dolby, baptised 17 May 1674, son of William D., fishmonger, admitted from St. James Clerkenwell October 1684; June 1689 to the Hudson Bay Company to be sent to H.B.

James Mires, baptised 5 December 1675, son of James M., admitted from St. James Clerkenwell 4 November 1684; 5 October 1692 to Edmond Drake, commander of the *Amity* bound for Barbados.

Admissions in April 1685

Samuell Smith, born 8 July 1677, son of Samuell S., framework knitter, admitted from St. Bride's; 10 November 1691 to his sister Sarah Underhill and Micajah Perry, merchant, to serve William Edwards, Clerk of the Council in Virginia.

Samuell Hinton, baptised 17 April 1678, son of Timothy H., merchant tailor, admitted from Hampton Wick, Middlesex; 31 January 1693 to his mother Mary Hinton and Mr. George Richards, citizen and weaver, to serve John Lane of York River, Virginia.

Thompson Hayne, born 16 August 1677, son of Thomas H., admitted from St. Michael Cornhill; 20 November 1691 to his said father and Micajah Perry, merchant, to serve Capt. John Lane of York River, Virginia, merchant.

Samuell Chaddock, born 24 February 1678, son of Richard C., admitted from St. Andrew Hubbard; 31 October 1694 to Humphry Ayler, commander of the *Jeffrey* bound for Jamaica.

Nathaniell Crockford, born 26 February 1675, son of Luke C., dyer, admitted from St. Saviour Southwark; 26 June 1688 to his mother Rebecca Crockford to go with Mr. Thomas Brinley, merchant, to Boston, New England.

Robert Jenkins, born 10 January 1676, son of Robert J., weaver, admitted from St. Olave Jewry; 11 May 1691 to his brother Jeremiah Jenkins to be bound to Francis Bond Esq. of Barbados, merchant.

Benjamin Langley, born 15 July 1676, son of Daniel L., barber surgeon, admitted from St. Dunstan in the West; 13 February 1692 to his friend Mr. Edmond Lightfoot and Micajah Perry, merchant, to serve Col. James Powell of James River, Virginia, merchant.

Admissions in April 1686

William Wright, born 1 September 1674, son of Robert W., admitted from Chiswick; 2 January 1690 to his cousin William Skelton to serve Daniel Park of York River, Virginia, merchant.

Nicholas Weeden, born 26 January 1675, son of Nicholas W., mason, admitted from Holy Trinity; June 1689 to Hudson Bay Company to be sent to H.B.

Humphrey Baldwin, born 10 May 1679, son of Humphrey B., vintner, admitted from St. Bride's; 22 January 1694 to Peter Dickary living in Bermondsey, Master of the *Hopewell* bound for Barbados.

John Whittorne, born 24 June 1679, son of Giles W., innholder, admitted from St. Foster's, London; 6 November 1690 to his mother Ruth Whittorne and Mr. Thomas Lane of St. Katherine Creechurch, merchant, to serve Col. James Powell in Virginia.

Admissions in April 1687

William Parsons, born 15 February 1675, son of William P., merchant tailor, admitted from St. Anne in the Fields;

12 November 1690 to Mr. John Blaxtone, apothecary in Newgate Market, and Richard Bell, citizen and haberdasher, on Ludgate Hill, to serve Capt. William Matthews, merchant at Port Royal, Jamaica.

James Newman, baptised 24 April 1680, son of Benjamin N., merchant tailor, admitted from St. Botolph Aldgate; 22 December 1695 to his mother Ellinor Newman to serve Edward Mitchell of London, merchant, in Jamaica.

Edward Jones, born 6 August 1673, son of Edward J., brewer, admitted from St. Botolph Aldersgate; 14 October 1691 to Robert Bell, commander of the *Chesterfield* bound for Jamaica.

John Chidley, baptised 3 August 1677, son of John C., cooper, admitted from St. Clement Danes; 10 November 1691 to his father John Chidley and Micajah Perry of London, merchant, to serve William Bird Esq. of James River, merchant.

Edward Audley, admitted by special order of Court; 22 April 1696 to Thomas Graves, commander of the *America* bound for Virginia. [Sarah Audley admitted at same time but died in February 1690].

James Walters, born 15 May 1677, son of John W., feltmaker, admitted from St. Anne Blackfriars; 2 December 1691 to his mother Ellinor Walters and Micajah Perry, merchant, to serve Major Arthur Allen of James River, Virginia, surveyor.

Admissions in April 1688

John Frognall, born 15 January 1679, son of Joseph F., barber surgeon, admitted from St. Dunstan Stepney; 6 November 1693 to his grandmother Margaret Birt to serve John Breholt, commander of the *New Exchange* bound for Barbados.

Marmaduke How, baptised 16 January 1680, son of Marmaduke H., joiner, admitted from Hackney; 21 July

1697 to Samuell Phillips, commander of the *Baltimore* bound for Virginia.

Benjamin Bridges, baptised 7 January 1678, son of Benjamin B., cutler, admitted from St. Botolph Aldgate; 7 April 1693 to John Morris, mariner, to serve him in New York with the consent of his friends.

Christopher Smith, baptised 25 January 1679, son of William S., admitted from St. Margaret Westminster; 10 November 1694 to his friend Hugh Squire Esq. and Ralph Marshall of St. Paul Covent Garden Esq. to serve Sir Edmond Andrews, Governor of Virginia.

William Foster, baptised 11 December 1687, son of Thomas F., cordwainer, admitted from [blank]; 22 April 1696 to John Brooke, commander of the *Joseph* bound for Jamaica.

Richard Smith, born 18 June 1681, son of Richard S., stationer, admitted from St. Katherine Coleman Street; 8 May 1696 to his uncle Abraham Jordan at College Hill to be bound to his uncle Nicholas Smith, commander of a ship bound for Virginia.

Isaac Browne, born 15 April 1679, son of Isaac B., apothecary, admitted from Wapping; 27 November 1691 to his grandmother Joane Underhill to serve George Polegreen of York River, Virginia.

Admissions in April 1689

Thomas Costine, baptised 20 August 1682, son of Edward C., innholder, admitted from St. Sepulchre; 28 May 1698 to Francis Rogers, commander of the *Castle* frigate bound for Jamaica.

John Cheese, born 25 March 1682, son of John C., joiner, admitted from Stepney; 6 November 1693 to John Breholt, commander of the *New Exchange* bound for Barbados.

Admissions in April 1690

Thomas Graven, baptised 22 October 1682, son of Thomas G., plumber, admitted from Putney, Surrey; 13 December 1699 to James England, commander of the *Tryon* bound for Barbados.

John Draycott, born 17 October 1681, son of John D., carman, admitted from St. Giles Cripplegate; December 1695 to his mother Mary D. to serve John Tills, Mr. of the *Mary* of Colchester bound for Barbados.

Benjamin Mills, baptised 15 January 1683, son of Thomas M., admitted from St. James Clerkenwell; 28 June 1699 to James Smith, commander of the *Sedgwick* bound for Jamaica.

Charles Reiley, born 20 April 1684, son of Charles R., admitted from St. Giles Cripplegate; 7 December 1700 to Richard Griffin, commander of the *Martha* bound for Barbados.

Admissions in April 1691

Luke Porter, baptised 18 November 1683, son of Luke Porter, pewterer, admitted from St. Margaret New Fish Street; 2 November 1700 to Joseph Pulman, commander of the *Hunter* bound for Jamaica.

Nathaniell Anthony, baptised 25 November 1683, son of John A., waterman, admitted from Deptford, Kent; 24 May 1701 to John Tickner, commander of the *Laurel* bound for Jamaica.

Thomas Knight, baptised 23 July 1682, son of Thomas K., cooper, admitted from St. Andrew Holborn; 21 January 1698 to Micajah Perry to serve Hon. William Bird of James River, Virginia.

Richard Crompton, baptised 28 October 1683, son of Richard C., fishmonger, admitted from St. Margaret Westminster; 27 October 1698 to his mother Anne Crompton and Benjamin Woolley, merchant in Mincing Lane, to serve Major Beverley of Gloucester Co., Virginia.

Stephen Clarke, born 2 August 1682, son of Hallalujah C., haberdasher, admitted from St. Martin in the Fields;

21 January 1698 to his friend James Kirby and Micajah Perry, merchant in Leadenhall Street, to serve Mr. Robert Beverley of James City, Virginia.

William King, born 15 February 1682, son of Edward C., clothworker, admitted from St. Leonard Shoreditch; 8 December 1697 to Samuell Phillips, commander of the *Catherine* bound for Jamaica.

Admissions in April 1692

John Watson, born 5 August 1683, son of John W., haberdasher, admitted from St. Katherine Creechurch; ?December 1698 to Micajah Perry, merchant in Leadenhall Street, to serve him in Virginia with the consent of his father-in-law Peter Griffith.

George Hale, baptised 17 December 1682, son of George H., wax chandler, admitted from St. Bartholomew the Great; 14 December 1698 to Bartholomew Whitehorne, commander of the [blank] bound for Virginia.

George Ruddle, baptised 28 September 1684, son of Richard R., vintner, admitted from St. Saviour Southwark; May 1702 to Jonas Mott, commander of the *Crow* bound for Virginia.

Abraham Paternoster, baptised 1 March 1686, son of Abraham P., weaver, admitted from Stepney; 8 August 1701 to his mother Anne Paternoster to serve James Cowes of St. Michael's Town, Barbados, councillor at law.

John White, born 26 February 1682, son of Thomas W., haberdasher, admitted from St. Saviour Southwark; 28 May 1698 to Michaell Staples, commander of the *Hopewell* bound for the West Indies.

Bartholomew Tatham, baptised 2 March 1684, son of Christopher T., haberdasher, admitted from St. Augustine; 14 November 1698 to his aunt Mary Tatham to serve Philip French of New York City, merchant.

Jonathan Lydyard, baptised 1 February 1685, son of William L., lorriner, admitted from St. Botolph Aldgate; 24 May 1701 to

Robert Ranson, commander of the *Golden Lyon* bound for Virginia and the West Indies. 24 May 1701.

Thomas Case, born 11 December 1680, son of John C., merchant tailor, admitted from St. Saviour Southwark; 22 April 1696 to Robert Lurting, commander of the *James* bound for Virginia.

Lionell Wood, born 19 January 1685, son of Robert W., glazier, admitted from St. Giles Cripplegate; 24 October 1702 to James Jackson, commander of the *Industry* bound for Barbados.

Admissions in April 1693

William Copson, baptised 15 April 1683, son of Moses C., cooper, admitted from St. Olave Hart Street; 4 February 1700 to Thomas Harrison, commander of the *Ashurst* bound for Jamaica.

Thomas King, born 14 October 1682, son of Peter K., ironmonger, admitted from St. Martin Ironmonger Lane; 14 December 1698 to Thomas Leman, commander of the *Isabella, Anne & Katherine* bound for Barbados.

William Colledge, baptised 2 November 1684, son of John C., cutler, admitted from Christchurch, London; 24 May 1701 to Joseph Peacock, commander of the *Bird* bound for Virginia.

John Gynes, baptised 8 December 1685, son of Edmond G., skinner, admitted from St. Saviour Southwark; October 1702 to Joseph Pulman, commander of the *Hunter* bound for Barbados.

Peter Hincks, baptised 6 February 1685, son of Peter H., clothworker, admitted from St. Andrew Undershaft; 24 May 1701 to William Cooper, commander of the *Jeffreys* bound for Virginia.

Admissions in April 1694

Isaac Elby, baptised 20 December 1685, son of John E., brewer, admitted from Stepney; 24 October 1702 to serve James Greenwell, commander of the *James* bound for Virginia.

George Barwick, baptised 6 September 1686, son of George B., joiner, admitted from St. Botolph Aldgate; 24 October 1702 to Thomas Crowforth, commander of the *Africa* bound for Virginia.

Frederick Vincent, baptised 18 April 1686, son of John V., admitted from St. Anne Blackfriars; October 1701 to John Keeling, churchwarden of St. Anne's, to go to James River, Virginia, with John Owen, merchant, now lodging with his father in Tower Street.

Admissions 1697/1698

Michaell Carver, baptised 20 September 1686, son of Michaell C., baker, admitted from St. Anne Blackfriars 10 May 1697; 27 February 1702 to John Keeling (as above) to serve John Foster of Boston, New England, mariner.

Richard Bragby, baptised 9 July 1691, son of Richard B., blacksmith, admitted from St. Dunstan in the East July 1698; January 1707 to his mother Elizabeth B. and Micajah Perry Esq. to serve Robert Carter Esq. of Rappahannock River, Virginia, merchant.

Admissions in April 1701

Thomas Wilson, born 22 November 1689, son of Thomas W., cooper, admitted from Stepney; November 1704 to his said father to serve John Marshall of Spanish Town, Jamaica.

Stephen Pike, born 19 December 1691, son of Stephen P., joiner, admitted from St. Giles Cripplegate; June 1705 to John Tasker of Maryland, merchant, with the consent of his aunt Jane Hopkins.

Caleb Austin, baptised 3 December 1689, son of Robert A., barber surgeon, admitted from St. James Duke's Place; February 1706 to John Ewer, fishmonger, and Benjamin

Bradley, merchant of London, to serve Capt. James Bray in James River, Virginia, merchant.

Thomas Wilson, born 14 March 1692, son of Thomas W., weaver, admitted from St. Giles Cripplegate; August 1707 to Micajah Perry Esq. to serve Mr. Thomas Read in Gloucester Co., York River, Virginia.

Admissions in April 1702

James Smith, baptised 29 July 1696, son of Nicholas S., innholder, admitted from St. Andrew Holborn; January 1711 to his friend Ambrose Milway and John Serocold, merchant in the Poultry, to serve Capt. Francis James in Port Royal, Jamaica, merchant.

Justice Child, baptised 27 January 1695, son of John C., shipwright, admitted from St. Mary Mounthaw; ?March 1711 to James Menzies of Boston, New England, counsellor.

Thomas Patrickson, born 8 May 1694, son of Joseph P., baker, admitted from St. Martin Ludgate; March 1709 to his mother Elizabeth P. and Micajah Perry Esq. to serve Hon. William Churchill in Rappahannock River, Virginia.

Admissions in April 1703

Gerrard Stamp, baptised 3 December 1693, son of William S., apothecary, admitted from St. Andrew Holborn; April 1709 with the consent of his grandmother to Micajah Perry Esq. to serve Mr. Nathaniell Burwell, Naval Officer of York River, Virginia.

Admissions in April 1704

William Hemming, born 2 February 1696, son of Richard H., framework knitter, admitted from Ham, Kingston, Surrey,; December 1710 to his aunt Mary Williams and John Phillips, cook in Cornhill, to serve Col. John Willis of Kingston, Jamaica, merchant.

Hannah Taylor, born 28 February 1698, daughter of Thomas T., cordwainer, admitted from St. James Clerkenwell; November 1709 to Mrs. Mary Whaley of Leadenhall Street, widow, to go with and serve her in Williamsburg, York River, Virginia.

Richard Fletcher, baptised 15 October 1696, son of Richard F., girdler, admitted from St. Mary Abchurch; January 1712 to Micajah Perry Esq. to serve Maj. Nathaniell Burrall of York River, Virginia, Collector of Customs.

James Mayott, baptised 9 August 1691, son of John M., merchant tailor, admitted from St. Botolph Bishopsgate; October 1706 to his aunt Elizabeth M. to serve Mr. Hugh Gaine, agent for sick and wounded seamen in Kingston, Jamaica.

Daniel Paxton, baptised 18 February 1694, son of Benjamin P., haberdasher, admitted from Christ Church; April 1709 to his mother Mary P. to serve Mr. Henry Rose, citizen and goldsmith of London, living in Jamaica.

Phillip Atherton, baptised 19 April 1696, son of Phillip A., admitted from Hammersmith; December 1713 to Raithwaith Barton, Mr. of the *Owners Adventure* bound for the West Indies.

Richard Allen, baptised 27 February 1696, son of Anthony A., butcher, admitted from St. Sepulchre; 19 January 17— to his cousin Elizabeth Scondred to be apprenticed to Molford Crow Esq. of Barbados, merchant.

Admissions in April 1705

Charles Adams, born 11 August 1697, son of Henry A., plasterer, admitted from St. Lawrence Jewry; September 1712 to his mother Suzan A. to serve Mr. Charles Carroll of Maryland, merchant.

Richard Colwall, baptised 15 September 1698, son of John C., founder, admitted from St. Andrew Holborn; 12 March 1714 to Samuel Tomlinson and Samuel Salmon to serve

George Lascelles of Barbados, merchant.

William Harrison, born 4 February 1697, son of William H., butcher, admitted from St. Botolph Aldgate; January 1712 to his mother Elizabeth H. to serve William Nicholson of South River, Maryland, merchant.

George Garth, baptised 6 October 1697, son of Roger G., shipwright, admitted from Fulham; December 1712 to his brothers Alexander and Roger G. and Micajah Perry Esq. to serve Phillip Ludlow Esq. of Virginia, merchant.

William Dodd, baptised 25 September 1696, son of George D., joiner, admitted from St. Giles in the Fields; November 1712 to Anthony Madden, commander of the *Robert & Francis* bound for Jamaica.

Thomas Stewart, born 15 December 1697, son of William S., innholder, admitted from St. Olave Hart Street; 4 December 1714 to William Cook, Mr. of the *Dove* bound for Antigua.

William Good, baptised 4 January 1697, son of Robert G., grocer, admitted from Enfield; February 1712 to his mother Lucy Good alias Wyatt and Mr. Henry Sheppard to serve Mr. James Knipe of Kingston, Jamaica, merchant.

Admissions in April 1706

Phillip Rudsby, born 5 March 1697, son of James R., fishmonger, admitted from St. James Westminster; March 1712 to his said father to serve Richard Harris of Boston, New England, mariner.

Isaac Sumner, baptised 17 February 1697, son of George S., bricklayer, admitted from St. Ethelburga; 7 November 1713 to Henry Sherburne, Master of the *Sophia* bound for New England.

Joseph Mepham, born 12 July 1699, son of Joseph M., haberdasher, admitted from St. Faith; 30 November 1715 to Richard Presman, Mr. of the *Dragon* bound for Jamaica.

Joseph Yorke, baptised 12 December 1697, son of John Y., merchant tailor, admitted from St. Botolph Aldgate; August 1712 to his said father and Mrs. Sarah Gresham to serve her husband, Mr. John Gresham, merchant in Maryland.

Gilbert Harvey, baptised 18 September 1698, son of Henry H., framework knitter, admitted from St. Mary le Bow; June 1715 to William Finch, Mr. of the frigate *Parker* bound for Boston, New England.

Jonah Bayley, baptised 11 July 1698, son of Thomas B., tobacco pipe maker, admitted from St. Giles Cripplegate; 23 December 1713 to his said father and Charles Wrigleworth in Clements Lane to serve Charles Hougham of Antigua, merchant.

Richard Deane, born 2 September 1698, son of Richard D., weaver, admitted from St. Giles Cripplegate; January 1714 to John Bolling, merchant in Virginia.

John Jephcot, born 10 August 1693, son of William J., merchant tailor, admitted from St. James Westminster; 20 June 1707 to his mother Mary Nechills to serve Thomas Barrow, lawyer in Jamaica.

Richard Sanders, baptised 20 February 1697, son of Thomas S., blacksmith, admitted from Stepney; December 1712 to James Waldy, commander of the *Granville* bound for Barbados.

John Duncalfe, baptised 10 October 1697, son of Joseph D., brewer, admitted from St. Anne Blackfriars; March 1713 to his uncle John Eding and Christopher Prissick of London, merchant, to serve Capt. William Codrington of Antigua, merchant.

Christopher Gardner, born 17 October 1694, son of John G., cardmaker, admitted from St. Botolph Aldgate; February 1710 to his sister Jane G. and Mr. Benjamin Bradley, merchant, to serve Mr. Samuell Smith, merchant in James River, Virginia.

Admissions in April 1707

Benjamin Chandler, baptised 25 January 1701, son of Peter C., haberdasher, admitted from St. Andrew Wardrobe; 2 May 1716 to his mother Mary Block to serve Thomas Aram, Mr. of the galley *Jolliffe* bound for Boston, New England.

Thomas Morris, baptised 22 February 1700, son of Thomas M., skinner, admitted from St. Martin in the Fields; 24 June 1715 to his mother Mary M. and bound to Benjamin Bradley, merchant, to be apprenticed to Mr. William Randall in Virginia, merchant.

Samuel Parrett, baptised 2 July 1699, son of Samuel P., basketmaker, admitted from St. Dunstan Stepney; 25 February 1715 to his mother Elizabeth P. and Micajah Perry Esq. to serve Edward Lloyd Esq. of Maryland, merchant.

Samuel Grimes, born 15 November 1697, son of Samuel G., vintner, admitted from St. Giles Cripplegate; 6 November 1713 to his mother Alice G. to serve William Willard of London, merchant, in Port Royal, Jamaica.

Thomas Strong, born 10 May 1699, son of Timothy S., mason, admitted from St. Gregory by St. Paul; 26 May 1716 to Randall Burroughs, Mr. of the *Phoenix* bound for Barbados.

Joseph Streater, born 2 November 1699, son of Joseph S., stationer, admitted from St. Nicholas, Rochester, Kent,; November 1715 to Samuel Payne, Mr. of the *Florida* bound for the West Indies.

William Hatt, baptised 14 January 1697, son of Andrew H., plasterer, admitted from Stepney; January 1712 to his uncle Thomas Milner and Mr. Benjamin Bradley, merchant, to serve Maj. Nathaniel Harrison of James River, Virginia, merchant.

Thomas Taylor, baptised 6 March 1697, son of Benjamin T., feltmaker, admitted from St. Sepulchre; December 1714 to Thomas Smith, Mr. of the *Isabella & Mary* bound for Barbados.

Edmond Bush, baptised 8 March 1700, son of Edward B., stationer, admitted from St. Mary, Oxford,; 30 May 1716 to John Watkinson, Mr. of the *Providence* bound for Pennsylvania.

Thomas White, born 17 November 1701, son of John W., goldsmith, admitted from St. Giles Cripplegate; 14 August 1718 to his mother Margaret W. and Micajah Perry Esq. to serve Maj. Robert Bolling of James River, Maryland.

John Hacker, baptised 3 September 1699, son of Richard H., glazier, admitted from St. Sepulchre; December 1714 to his sister Martha H. and William Willard to serve Michael Dodd of Port Royal, Jamaica, merchant.

William Loader, baptised 14 February 1698, son of William Loader, joiner, admitted from St. Mary Mounthaw; December 1714 to Daniel Bright, Mr. of the *Tavistock* bound for Jamaica.

George Dickinson, baptised 2 October 1698, son of George D., needlemaker, admitted from St. Olave Southwark; 26 August 1714 to his aunt Margaret Smith to serve Henry Newton of Bridgetown, Barbados, merchant.

Joseph Sharp, born 25 October 1700, son of Joseph S., admitted from Christ Church; 10 September 1715 to his sister Mary S. to serve Thomas Sprigg of Putuxon River, Maryland, merchant.

Edward Bayley, baptised 10 April 1698, son of Richard B., fishmonger, admitted from St. Giles Cripplegate; 17 November 1713 to his mother Jane B. and Micajah Perry Esq. to serve John Rowsby? Esq. of Putuxon River, Maryland.

Admissions in April 1708

John Widenell, baptised 9 October 1702, son of Francis W., armourer, admitted from St. Sepulchre; 29 December 1718 to his mother Hester W. and Humphrey Bell of London, merchant, to serve Mr. James Walker of Virginia, merchant.

James Venable, born 6 May 1699, son of John V., haberdasher, admitted from St. Olave Silver Street; 18 December 1713 to his mother Hannah Earl to serve Colin Pratt of New Aberdeen, York River, Virginia, merchant.

Adrian Maidman, baptised 4 August 1701, son of John M., admitted from St. Botolph Bishopsgate; December 1715 to his aunt Ann Pinman to serve George Dunken of Bridge Town, Barbados.

James Batterton, baptised 14 December 1701, son of James B., embroiderer, admitted from St. Dunstan in the West; 25 October 1718 to Anthony Wilks, Mr. of the frigate *Backford* bound for Jamaica.

William Prentis, born 10 October 1699, son of John P., embroiderer, admitted from St. John Zachary; 4 November 1714 to his said father to serve Archibald Blaer of Williamsburg, Virginia, merchant.

John Proctor, born 20 September 1701, son of Edmond P., goldsmith, admitted from St. Mary Staining; 25 May 1717 to Richard Gibbons, Mr. of the *Association* bound for the West Indies.

Andrew Hilman, baptised 1 April 1700, son of Thomas H., leatherseller, admitted from St. Sepulchre; 28 September 1715 to his mother Alice H. and Micajah Perry Esq. to serve James Carroll of Annapolis, Maryland, merchant.

Admissions in April 1709

John Beck, born 15 December 1700, son of John B., admitted from Skellingthorpe, Lincs.; 28 September 1715 to Micajah Perry Esq. to serve Richard Bennett Esq. of Maryland, merchant.

Thomas Ashby, baptised 7 April 1700, son of Nicholas A., weaver, admitted from All Hallows Barking; 7 November 1716 to his said father to serve Daniel Smith Esq., Governor of Nevis.

Joseph Mathew, born 2 July 1700, son of William M.,

goldsmith, admitted from St. Mary Magdalene Milk Street; November 1715 to his mother Mary M. and Mr. Christopher Prissick to serve Col. William Coddrington of Antigua, merchant.

John Parry, born 21 July 1698, son of Owen P., dyer, admitted from St. James Garlickhithe; 30 October 1713 to his mother Mary P. and Micajah Perry Esq. to serve Robert Carter Esq. of Rappahannock, Virginia, merchant.

Samuell Hopkins, baptised 15 June 1701, son of Samuell H., turner, admitted from St. Andrew Holborn; May 1715 to his friend Sarah Dobbins to serve in Hudson's Bay.

Robert Biscoe, born 27 November 1699, son of John B., fishmonger, admitted from Holy Trinity; November 1716 to his mother Elizabeth Allen and Micajah Perry Esq. to serve Hon. Robert Carter of Rappahannock River, Virginia, merchant.

Robert Hoare, baptised 16 November 1701, son of George H., butcher, admitted from St. Mary Whitechapel; 30 April 1717 to his mother Elizabeth Hunt to serve Richard Beresford of South Carolina, merchant.

William Bird, baptised 8 February 1701, son of Thomas B., barber surgeon, admitted from St. Michael Wood Street with St. Mary Staining; 28 September 1715 to his mother Elizabeth B. and Mr. Christopher Beswick to serve Col. William Coddrington of Antigua, merchant.

John Cushee, baptised 25 August 1700, son of John C., innholder, admitted from St. James Clerkenwell; January 1715 to Joseph Foye, Mr. of the *Eagle* bound for New England.

Meager Green, born 10 July 1701, son of Francis G., admitted from Bridewell Precinct; 26 July 1716 to John Corney, Mr. of the *Elizabeth* bound for New England.

Burcomb Newman, baptised 5 February 1702, son of John N., barber surgeon, admitted from St. Mary Whitechapel; 16 October 1717 to his father-in-law John Gunbey and

Richard Chester of London, merchant, to serve Mr. Robert Moore of Barbados, merchant.

William Wheelehouse, baptised 20 April 1701, son of John W., shipwright, admitted from St. Olave Southwark; 25 May 1717 to James Belcher, Mr. of the *Port Nelson* bound for Hudson's Bay.

William Neale, baptised 13 October 1699, son of William N., joiner, admitted from St. Leonard Shoreditch; September 1714 to his mother Elizabeth N. and Francis Melmoth of London, merchant, to serve Dr. Owen of Kings Town, Jamaica, merchant.

James King, born 30 November 1699, son of John K., weaver, admitted from St. Clement Danes; 29 March 1715 to his mother Sarah K. and William Davis on behalf of his brother Richard Bill of Boston, New England, merchant, whom he is to serve.

Nathaniell Bridgman, baptised 2 April 1701, son of William B., poulterer, admitted from All Hallows Staining; 23 November 1707 to Samuell Roberts, Mr. of the *Althea* bound for Jamaica.

Henry Pratt, born 10 May 1702, son of Henry P., tiler, admitted from St. Botolph Aldgate; 9 October 1717 to his mother Elizabeth Prime and Mr. George Newport to serve Dr. James Bootman of Barbados.

Thomas Ellison, baptised 31 January 1696, son of Thomas E., carpenter, admitted from St. Andrew Undershaft; January 1712 to his mother Catherine E. to serve Jeremia Turner, Mr. of the *Spotswood* bound for Virginia.

John Parr, baptised - February 1702, son of John P., merchant tailor, admitted from St. Botolph Aldersgate; 28 September 1715 to his mother Tabitha P. and Micajah Perry Esq. to serve Phillip Lloyd Esq. of Maryland, merchant.

William Dickinson, baptised 22 July 1701, son of William D., haberdasher, admitted from St. Sepulchre; 20 February 1717 to his mother Margaret D. and Charles Wriglesworth on behalf of Mr. Nathaniell Carpenter of London, merchant, to serve William Grantum of Antigua.

John Randall, baptised 18 February 1700, son of Edmond R., feltmaker, admitted from St. Bride's; 9 April 1714 to the grandfather John Ellison to serve Dudley Woodbridge of Barbados, merchant.

John Niccoll, born 26 January 1701, son of Benjamin N., fishmonger, admitted from Whitechapel; June 1715 to Richard Read, Mr. of the *Crow* bound for Virginia.

James Lickorish, born 7 January 1703, son of James L., blacksmith, admitted from St. Botolph Aldersgate; 1 October 1718 to his mother and Mr. Joseph Macham of London, merchant, to serve Mr. Samuell Martin of Antigua, merchant.

Robert Driver, baptised 15 December 1699, son of Robert D., glover, admitted from St. Giles Cripplegate; 30 May 1716 to John Cunningham, Mr. of the *Crown* bound for Barbados.

Josiah Gosling, born 14 January 1701, son of Josiah G., cordwainer, admitted from St. Magnus Martyr; 25 May 1717 to George Berley, Mr. of the *Anthony* bound for Hudson's Bay.

John Plesto, born 23 April 1702, son of Thomas P., merchant tailor, admitted from St. Giles Cripplegate; 24 January 1717 to his said father and Mr. Christopher Prissick to serve Col. William Coddrington of Antigua, merchant.

Mathew Edward Thompson, baptised 18 September 1702, son of Edward T., admitted from Woodford, Essex in the place of John White; 25 June 1717 to the aunt Ann Shelley and John Bayeux living in Bishopsgate Street, to serve Mr. James Dupre of New York, schoolmaster.

Peter Ivers, baptised - February 1702, son of Peter I., cook, admitted from St. Botolph Aldersgate in the place of Samuell White; 4 October 1716 to James Roscow of York River, Virginia, merchant.

Admissions in April 1711

Francis Rosamond, baptised 18 March 1702, son of William R., framework knitter, admitted from St. John Hackney; 23 October 1716 to his mother Anne R. and William Parrot to serve Col. William Thomas of Antigua, merchant.

John Fryer, born 6 December 1702, son of Richard F., fruiterer, admitted from St. Martin Vintry; 7 November 1717 to the aunt Alce Nicholas to serve Mr. Hugh Hall Jr. of Barbados, merchant.

John Thatcher, born 19 April 1701, son of Thomas T., weaver, admitted from St. Giles Cripplegate; 1 June 1716 to his uncle William Kilner and Mr. Edward Bridgen of London, merchant, to serve Mr. Joseph Roswell of Barbados, merchant.

Jonathan Sherrer, born 21 June 1701, son of John S., cardmaker, admitted from St. Giles Cripplegate; 18 April 1716 to his mother Elizabeth S. and Mr. John Caswall to serve George Clark Esq. of New York, merchant.

Banfield Hearne, baptised 20 November 1698, son of John H., glasier, admitted from St. Leonard Shoreditch; 2 December 1713 to his mother Elizabeth H. to serve Robert Tucker of James River, Virginia, merchant.

John Brand, born 2 December 1702, son of John B., weaver, admitted from Stepney; 9 June 1718 to his mother Catherine B., and David Jerrard, weaver, to serve John Sampson of Barbados, merchant.

Zachariah Leigh, born 9 April 1704, son of John L., admitted from Carshalton, Surrey; August 1718 to his mother Sarah L. and Micajah Perry Esq. to serve James Roscow of Virginia, merchant.

Robert Ball, baptised 15 June 1701, son of John B., shipwright, admitted from St. Saviour Southwark; December 1716 to his said father to serve Benjamin Hall of Barbados, merchant.

William Grainger, born 11 March 1701, son of John G., merchant tailor, admitted from St. Giles Cripplegate; March 1716 to his mother Mary G. to serve John Yeomans of Barbados, merchant.

John Prigg, baptised 9 March 1701, son of Mathew P., admitted from St. James Duke's Place; May 1717 to his mother Mary P. to serve Thomas Dansie, Mr. of the *Bewdley* bound for Barbados.

Phillip Raymond, baptised 20 March 1701, son of Thomas R., mercer, admitted from St. Bride's; 5 October 1718 to Thomas Smith, Mr. of the *Isabella & Mary* bound for Barbados.

John Smith, baptised 27 May 1702, son of Thomas S., joiner, admitted from St. Leonard Shoreditch; 28 February 1718 to his mother Sarah S. to serve Francis Burton of Antigua, merchant.

James Surridge, baptised 6 December 1702, son of John S., brewer, admitted from St. Leonard Shoreditch; 13 May 1719 to William Greenwood, Mr. of the *Margaret* bound for Virginia.

Ebinezer Meeres, born 15 August 1702, son of John M., feltmaker, admitted from St. Andrew Holborn; February 1717 to his mother Mary M. and Abraham Gibbon, merchant living in Coleman Street, to serve William Gibbon of Kings Town, Jamaica.

William Amey, born 23 February 1704, son of William A., joiner, admitted from All Hallows Bread Street; 20 March 1719 to his friend William Norris to serve Caleb Lindall of Barbados, merchant.

Richard Kester, born 13 June 1702, son of Richard K., barber surgeon, admitted from St. Lawrence Pountney; 12 August 1718 to his mother Elizabeth K. to serve Thomas Sanders, Mr. of the frigate *Kingstown* bound for Jamaica.

John Blundall, baptised 25 May 1702, son of Edward B., weaver, admitted from St. Mary Newington, Surrey; 22 February

1718 to his aunt Mrs. Mary Wright and Mr. John Faulkner to serve Mr. Gilbert Falconar of Maryland, merchant.

Mary Baker, baptised 2 February 1703, daughter of Robert B., gunmaker, admitted from St. Botolph Aldgate; February 1717 to her mother Susannah B. and Edward Byam of London, merchant, to serve Edward Byam Esq., Governor of Antigua.

George Whitlidge, born 9 July 1703, son of Daniel W., stationer, admitted from St. Martin Ludgate; 14 January 1718 to his uncle Robert W. and Mr. Robert Cary of London, merchant, to serve Mr. John Baylor of Virginia, merchant.

Adam Jellicoe, baptised 9 May 1702, son of Adam J., weaver, admitted from St. Leonard Shoreditch; 3 October 1718 to his cousin Adam J. to serve Mr. John Barbottain of Antigua, merchant.

Thomas Clark, baptised 17 November 1703, son of Thomas C., distiller, admitted from St. Olave Southwark; October 1719 to Thomas Auborie, Mr. of the *James & Mary* bound for Barbados.

Charles Daniel, born 11 May 1703, son of Charles D., goldsmith, admitted from St. Giles Cripplegate; December 1717 to his sister Mary Dunbar and Micajah Perry Esq. to serve Hon. Charles Carroll of Maryland, merchant.

William Wyatt, baptised 27 September 1702, son of William W., leatherseller, admitted from St. Andrew by the Wardrobe; November 1716 to George Jesson, Mr. of the galley *Sarah* bound for Jamaica.

Charles Boote, baptised 2 August 1703, son of Joseph B., haberdasher, admitted from St. Sepulchre; December 1717 to his cousin Ann Pell and Micajah Perry Esq. to serve James Heath Esq. of Maryland, merchant.

Thomas Crouch, born 9 November 1700, son of Thomas C., plasterer, admitted from St. Giles Cripplegate; September 1718 to his said father and Micajah Perry Esq. to serve

Edward Lloyd Esq. of Maryland, merchant.

Robert Massey, born in November 1702, son of John M., goldsmith, admitted from Christ Church; November 1717 to his uncle Isaac M. to serve Robert Mears, Mr. of the *Prince Alexander* bound for Jamaica.

Gilbert Griffin, baptised 5 July 1702, son of Joseph G., carpenter, admitted from St. Peter Paul's Wharf; 23 November 1717 to John Harray, Mr. of the *Boynator* bound for the West Indies.

William Shrimpton, born 3 April 1702, son of Richard S., plasterer, admitted from St. Michael le Querne; [no date] to his brother Richard S. and Micajah Perry Esq. to serve Robert Mumford of James River, merchant.

John Cason, baptised 21 December 1701, son of Isaac C., glasier, admitted from St. Andrew Undershaft; 27 May 1718 to John Hutton, Mr. of the *Princes Galley* bound for Barbados.

William Ridout, baptised 9 October 1700, son of Richard R., admitted from Sherborne, Dorset, in the place of John Pitman; 25 February 1716 to his friend William Lambert to serve Adino Bullfinch of Boston, New England, sailmaker.

Richard Bowen, baptised 9 April 1704, son of Walwin B., fishmonger, admitted from St. Mary le Bow in place of William Bully; 21 August 1719 to his said father and Mr. George Newport of London, merchant, to serve Hon. George Walker of Barbados.

William Kemp, baptised 20 January 1706, son of William K., innholder, admitted from St. Stephen Coleman Street in the place of Thomas Benford deceased; 13 October 1719 to his mother Elizabeth Claridge and Capt. Marmaduke Paine to serve Mr. John Huffam of Nevis, merchant.

Henry Shepherd, born 31 January 1705, son of Mathew S., skinner, admitted from St. Thomas Apostle in the place of Joseph Jones; 30 November 1721 to John Smyter, Mr. of the galley *Carolina* bound for Carolina.

Admissions in April 1714

John Hall, baptised 30 July 1706, son of Richard H., paviour, admitted from All Hallows London Wall; 28 July 1721 to his uncle John H. and Thomas Trueman living in Broad Street, to serve John Downe of Nevis, merchant.

Edward Brown, born 24 December 1706, son of Thomas B., joiner, admitted from St. Benet Paul's Wharf; March 1721 to his friend Mary Bray and Mr. Healy Harris, Mr. of the *Endeavour* to serve Mr. Henry Lawrance of Barbados, merchant.

Daniel Peterson, born 13 November 1707, son of Thomas P., joiner, admitted from Stepney; 5 March 1722 to his mother Sarah P. and Mr. John Yaldwyn living at Chapel House, London Bridge, to serve Phillip Redwood of Spanish Town, Jamaica, merchant.

Sotherne Nash, born 2 March 1702, son of John N., framework knitter, admitted from Liberty of Norton Folgate; 20 February 1717 to Archibald Cockram of Antigua, merchant.

William Yockkins, baptised 5 December 1705, son of John Y., plasterer, admitted from All Hallows London Wall; 10 May 1720 to his said father and Mr. James Butler of London, merchant, to serve Col. Thomas Butler of Nevis, merchant.

Josias Goodman, born 25 November 1704, son of John G., clothworker, admitted from St. Lawrence Pountney; June 1720 to Richard Shubrick, Mr. of the *Hopewell* bound for South Carolina.

Richard Clarke, baptised 29 October 1704, son of Robert C., weaver, admitted from St. Botolph Bishopsgate; 1 October 1718 to his mother Elinor Ames and Micajah Perry Esq. to serve John Pratt of Virginia, merchant.

Thomas Jacombe, baptised 14 March 1707, son of Nehemiah J., feltmaker, admitted from St. Faith under St. Paul's; 28 June 1722 to his mother Ann J. and John Davy Breholt of London, merchant, to serve Matthew Guignan of St. Christopher's, merchant.

William Cooper, baptised 14 September 1704, son of William C., carpenter, admitted from St. Michael Bassishaw; 10 July 1718 to his father-in-law Edward Brimbley and Mr. Benjamin Bradley of London, merchant, to serve Capt. Henry Harrison of Virginia, merchant.

William Stone Francklin, baptised 5 January 1704, son of Phillip F., leatherseller, admitted from St. Clement Danes; July 1720 to his brother Charles F. to serve William Ryder, Mr. of the galley *Fanteen* bound for Guinea and Barbados.

Jacob Ward, baptised 4 February 1705, son of Jacob W., cooper, admitted from St. Saviour Southwark; October 1720 to his mother Ursula W. to serve John Levett, Mr. of the *Martha* bound for America.

William Sired, baptised 4 February 1705, son of Randall S., haberdasher, admitted from St. Stephen Coleman Street; 4 May 1720 to his said father to serve John Hext, Mr. of the *Charles Town* bound for South Carolina.

John Woobanck, baptised 7 July 1706, son of John W., haberdasher, admitted from St. Mary Whitechapel; 27 November 1721 to his cousin Elinor Vickery to serve Mr. John Pratt of Virginia, merchant.

William Flower, baptised 24 September 1704, son of John F., poulterer, admitted from St. Katherine Coleman; 6 March 1719 to his mother Jane F. and William Mathew to serve Penelope Mead, widow, of St. Christopher's.

William Pack, baptised 24 April 1703, son of John P., dyer, admitted from St. John Baptist; 27 July 1717 to his uncle Richard Day to serve Stephen Yeakley, Mr. of the *Annapolis* bound for Maryland.

George Adams, baptised 30 May 1704, son of John A., joiner, admitted from St. Clement Danes; February 1719 to his cousin Henry Bradshaw and Samuel Baker of London, merchant, to serve Mr. Robert Jenney of New York, schoolmaster.

Nathaniel Goudge, baptised 7 September 1701, son of Richard G., painter stainer, admitted from St. Mary Whitechapel; April 1717 to his brother William G. to serve Samuel Boyles, Mr. of the *Dunwich Merchant* bound for Guinea and Jamaica.

William Stevens, baptised 19 March 1704, son of Richard S., plasterer, admitted from St. Bartholomew the Less; March 1719 to his mother Sarah S. to serve Caleb Lindall of Barbados, merchant.

John Hurst, baptised 7 April 1706, son of William H., joiner, admitted from Holy Trinity; April 1721 to his friend Matthew Butterwick and Thomas Tryon to serve Col. James Elliott of Barbados, merchant.

Nicholas Westell, baptised 26 August 1705, son of Francis W., admitted from Richmond, Surrey; January 1721 to his friend Mary Spike and Mr. William Tryon Jr. of London, merchant, to serve Francis Carlile Esq. of Antigua, merchant.

Thomas Clarke, born 29 January 1706, son of Thomas C., fruiterer, admitted from Christ Church; 23 January 1720 to Mr. Richard Cope of London, merchant, to serve Mr. John Woodley of Nevis, merchant.

Eleanor Cheynee, baptised 31 January 1705, daughter of Thomas C., barber surgeon, admitted from St. Faith under St. Paul's; February 1717 to her mother Mary C. and Mr. Christopher Prissick of London, merchant, to serve the daughter of Col. Edward Byam in Antigua.

George Bartholomew, baptised 18 September 1703, son of Thomas B., goldsmith, admitted from St. Bride's; December 1720 to Andrew Joad, Mr. of the *New Mitford* bound for Maryland.

Thomas Underwood, baptised 6 February 1705, son of John U., clothworker, admitted from St. Giles Cripplegate; 20 November 1719 to his mother Joane U. and Mr. Humphrey Bell of London, merchant, to serve Mr. Phillip Whitehead of Virginia, merchant.

John Ashby, baptised 23 March 1704, son of Timothy A., carman, admitted from St. Olave Southwark; 12 December 1718 to his friend John Taylor and Mr. Francis Melmoth of London, merchant, to serve Claudius Archbould of Jamaica, merchant.

Admissions in April 1715

Nathaniel Giles, baptised 27 May 1704, son of Nathaniel G., shipwright, admitted from St. Bartholomew the Less; 21 July 1719 to his aunt Sarah Henley to serve Nicholas Trott of Bermuda, merchant.

Benjamin Ferdinando, baptised 15 January 1707, son of Isaac F., blacksmith, admitted from St. Peter Paul's Wharf; 17 December 1720 to his mother Mary F. and Micajah Perry Esq. to serve Francis Epes of Virginia, merchant.

John Smith, baptised 9 December 1705, son of Robert S., leatherseller, admitted from St. Gregory by St. Paul; 17 December 1720 to his mother Elizabeth S. and Micajah Perry Esq. to serve James Roscow of Virginia, merchant.

Richard Hyde, baptised 28 March 1705, son of James H., barber surgeon, admitted from Whitefriars Precinct; 13 February 1721 to his uncle Henry H. to serve Capt. Francis Willis of Virginia, merchant.

John Davis, born 19 July 1705, son of William D., clothworker, admitted from St. Saviour Southwark; 13 December 1721 to John Cobb, Mr. of the *Willis* bound for Virginia.

Joseph Styth, baptised 16 February 1707, son of Farrainbrace S., merchant tailor, admitted from St. Giles in the Fields; 13 July 1721 to his sister Ann Rayner and Marmaduke Payne, mariner, to serve John Huffam of Nevis, merchant.

Thomas Williams, baptised 22 February 1707, son of George W., carman, admitted from St. Olave Southwark; 26 May 1723 to his mother Hannah W. to serve Edward Jones of Bermuda, merchant.

Michael Hartley, born 23 October 1705, son of Michael H., joiner, admitted from St. Olave Old Jewry; 22 October 1719 to his mother Lydia H. to serve Samuel Fry of Antigua, merchant.

Henry Ayres, baptised 30 January 1707, son of William A., tallow chandler, admitted from St. Mary Whitechapel; 15 June 1723 to William Bell, Mr. of the *Sallymander* bound for Bermuda.

Robert Browne, baptised 27 January 1705, son of Robert B., cutler, admitted from St. Dunstan in West; November 1718 to his mother Hester B. and Richard Coope of London, salter, to serve Mrs. Hester Penheiava of Nevis, merchant.

Richard Cooker, baptised 6 March 1706, son of Thomas C., carman, admitted from St. Mary Whitechapel; 24 September 1719 to his mother Margaret C. to serve John Willett of St. Christopher's.

John Stevens, baptised 19 August 1705, son of Richard S, loriner, admitted from St. Olave Hart Street; 8 October 1720 to his mother-in-law Jane Crump to serve Mr. Edward Spencer of St. Christopher's.

John Fletcher, baptised 3 April 1705, son of John F., haberdasher, admitted from St. Botolph Aldgate; May 1720 to his mother Mary Wallband and Mr. James Butler of London, merchant, to serve Anthony and Peacock Walker of Nevis, merchants.

Robert Smith Woobanck, baptised 21 November 1703, son of John W., haberdasher, admitted from St. Mary Whitechapel; 30 October 1717 by the consent of his grandmother Elizabeth Smith to Mr. Benjamin Bradley, merchant, to serve Nathaniel Harrison Esq. of Virginia, merchant.

Robert Ashton, baptised 10 September 1704, son of Walter A., wire drawer, admitted from St. Botolph Aldersgate; 13 January 1720 to his mother Mary A. and Capt. John Smith to serve John Richardson Esq. of Nevis, merchant.

Richard Robinson, baptised 3 July 1706, son of William R., mercer, admitted from Esher, Surrey; January 1722 to his said father to serve James Gordon of St. Christopher's.

John Brett, born in August 1704, son of Charles B., merchant tailor, admitted from [blank]; November 1719 to his mother Catherine B. to serve Nathaniel Barnard, Mr. of the *Susanna* bound for Maryland.

Samuel Wilkinson, baptised 7 July 1706, son of Thomas W., upholder, admitted from St. Mary Aldermanbury; December 1720 to his mother Rachell W. and Micajah Perry Esq. to serve Archibald Blayer of Virginia, merchant.

William Pearce, born 1 July 1706, son of Francis P., joiner, admitted from St. Martin in the Fields; 17 March 1722 to his mother Mary Chapman and Phillip Smith of London, merchant, to serve Samuel Pool of Maryland, merchant.

John Edwards, born 5 January 1705, son of John E., joiner, admitted from St. Martin Ludgate; 29 November 1721 by the consent of his mother Elizabeth Cawthorne to Samuel Lancelott, Mr. of the galley *Haywood* bound for Jamaica.

William Jennings, baptised 11 February 1707, son of Andrew J., draper, admitted from Hampstead, Middlesex; 8 February 1725 to his uncle Henry Yates to serve Isaac Scarth, Mr. of the *Sea Horse* bound for Barbados.

William Champneys, baptised 9 June 1706, son of John C., feltmaker, admitted from St. Dunstan in West; December 1720 to his said father and Micajah Perry Esq. to serve Richard Chichester of Rappahannock River, Virginia, Collector of Customs.

Thomas Noon, baptised 23 September 1706, son of Jonas N., joiner, admitted from Sevenoaks, Kent; February 1721 to his mother Hannah N. to serve Mr. Nicholas Gallwey of St. Christopher's, merchant.

John More, baptised 9 February 1705, son of John M., pattenmaker, admitted from St. Margaret Westminster; 8 August 1719 to his said father and Mr. Richards Higginson of London, merchant, to serve Mr. Richard Splatt of South Carolina, merchant.

Richard Elliot, baptised 9 April 1704, son of Richard E., pattenmaker, admitted from St. Bride's; November 1717 to his mother Mary E. and Mr. John Smith to serve William Smith Esq. of St. Christopher's.

John Lepper, born 20 January 1705, son of Thomas L., butcher, admitted from St. Giles in the Fields; 4 September 1719 to his cousin Samuel Hawtyn to serve John Haden of St. Christopher's.

William Fenn, baptised 6 January 1706, son of William F., innholder, admitted from St. Botolph Bishopsgate; January 1720 to his mother Mary Manwood and Mr. Richard Coope of London, merchant, to serve Col. Charles Bridgewater of Nevis, merchant.

Thomas Morton, born 11 June 1707, son of Thomas M., founder, admitted from St. Giles Cripplegate; February 1723 to his aunt Ruth M. and Samuel Wragg of London, merchant, to serve Thomas Dunes of Charles City, South Carolina, merchant.

Christopher Simmonds, baptised 22 February 1708, son of Thomas S., admitted from St. Saviour Southwark; 23 July 1722 to his uncles William and George S. and to Mrs. Lucy Leaver to serve her husband Mr. William Leaver of Kingston, Jamaica, merchant.

Peter Upholfens, born 12 April 1708, son of John U., embroiderer, admitted from St. Giles in the Fields; February 1723 to his friend Thomas Thorn and Samuel Wragg to serve Thomas Murray of Barbados, merchant.

Isaac Rambow, baptised 7 September 1704, son of Isaac R., barber surgeon, admitted from St. Peter le Poor; 14 August 1718 to his uncle Nathaniel Berry and Micajah Perry Esq. to serve John Irwin of Virginia, merchant.

Isaac Game, baptised 23 January 1705, son of Abraham G., waterman, admitted from Harwich, Essex; 17 May 1721 to Joseph Smethurst, Mr. of the *King George* bound for the West Indies.

Thomas Headington, baptised 4 June 1704, son of Thomas H., blacksmith, admitted from St. Andrew Holborn; 20 January 1719 to his mother-in-law Elizabeth Egglestone and Mr. Samuel Wragg of London, merchant, to serve his brother Mr. Jos. Wragg of Charles Town, South Carolina.

George Marshall, baptised 11 June 1704, son of John M., armourer, admitted from St. Mary Whitechapel; 15 February 1720 to his uncle Mr. Joseph Brown and Mr. Nathaniel Barnardiston of London, merchant, to serve Gilles McArther of St. Christopher's, merchant.

John Fisher, baptised 15 June 1707, son of Caesar F., joiner, admitted from St. Giles in the Fields; 28 June 1722 to his sister Elizabeth F. and John Davy Breholt of London, merchant, to serve Benjamin King of St. Christopher's, merchant.

George Dennis, born 11 October 1705, son of John D., joiner, admitted from St. Dunstan Stepney; January 1721 to his mother Frances D. and Mr. Humphrey Bell of London, merchant, to serve Mr. James Walker of Rappahannock River, Virginia, merchant.

Edward Fenton, baptised 27 November 1704, son of Edward F., weaver, admitted from St. Katherine by the Tower; 18 March 1719 to his mother Elizabeth F. to serve Mr. Daniel Allen & Co. of London in Jamaica.

James Hudson, baptised 12 November 1704, son of Robert H., merchant tailor, admitted from St. Andrew Holborn;

15 September 1721 to his grandmother Sarah H. to serve Martin Salter, Mr. of the *Griffin* bound for Barbados.

James Castle, born 25 July 1705, son of Daniel C., loriner, admitted from St. Giles Cripplegate; 26 September 1720 to his mother Hannah C. and Mr. Thomas Trueman of London, merchant, to serve Michael Lambath Esq. of St. Christopher's, merchant.

Admissions in April 1716

Robert Carellis, baptised 8 September 1706, son of Robert C., haberdasher, admitted from St. Andrew Undershaft; 12 December 1720 to his uncle Rupert Ellcie and Micajah Perry Esq. to serve Col. Cole Diggs of Virginia, merchant.

Edward Armstrong, baptised 24 October 1708, son of John A., vintner, admitted from St. Mary Whitechapel; 13 November 1725 to Charles Hallifax, Mr. of the *Great Walpole* bound for St. Christopher's.

Daniel Whitworth, born 11 April 1707, son of Cornelius W., dyer, admitted from St. Mary Magdalene Bermondsey; 1 December 1721 to his mother Sarah W. and John Richardson of Bermondsey, mariner, to serve Isaac Thomas of St. Christopher's, merchant.

John Swallwell, baptised 26 October 1707, son of John S., loriner, admitted from St. Botolph Aldersgate; 16 April 1722 by the consent of his aunt Dorothy Styles to Mr. John Soden of London, merchant, to serve Archabel Cumming of New England, merchant.

Richard Keate, baptised 11 July 1708, son of John K., carman, admitted from St. Botolph Bishopsgate; — to Micajah Perry Esq. to serve Richard Bennett Esq. of Maryland, merchant.

Phillip Delamotte, baptised 28 November 1707, son of John D., fishmonger, admitted from St. Dunstan in the East; 10 June 1724 to Thomas Lance, Mr. of the *Diligence* bound for Antigua.

James Lake, born 20 March 1707, son of Henry L., coachmaker, admitted from St. Sepulchre; 3 August 1722 to his brother Henry Lake and Mr. Joseph Adams, merchant, to serve Col. John Burton of Antigua, merchant.

Henry Orfeur, born 6 August 1706, son of Thomas O., draper, admitted from Clapham, Surrey; 12 May 1720 to his mother Sarah O. and Mr. James Butler to serve Mr. James Symonds of Nevis, merchant.

Thomas Groves, baptised 16 July 1705, son of Samuel G., shipwright, admitted from St. Clement Danes; 23 June 1721 to his mother Johanna Harding to serve Abraham Vining, Mr. of the *Neptune* bound for Pennsylvania.

Thomas Banfield, born 10 June 1706, son of Richard B., clothworker, admitted from St. Saviour Southwark; 17 January 1721 to his mother Elizabeth B. and Mr. Nathaniel Carpenter of London, merchant, to serve Mr. Nathaniel Pilbert of Antigua, merchant.

William Peete, baptised 11 March 1707, son of Richard P., leatherseller, admitted from St. Mary Whitechapel; 18 January 1722 to his mother Margaret P. and Mr. Joseph Macham of London, merchant, to serve Col. Thomas Bedford of Jamaica, merchant.

Adrian Maidman, baptised 5 August 1705, son of Adrian M., weaver, admitted from St. Botolph Bishopsgate; 12 December 1720 to his mother Martha Faulkner and Micajah Perry Esq. to serve Richard Bennett Esq. of Maryland, merchant.

John Harvey, baptised 21 October 1707, son of John H., shipwright, admitted from St. Paul Shadwell; 5 July 1721 to his aunt Hannah Wood and Micajah Perry Esq. to serve [blank] of Virginia, merchant.

William Henry Terret, baptised 6 May 1707, son of Henry T., clothworker, admitted from All Hallows the Great; 17 December 1720 to his uncle Thomas Arne and Micajah Perry Esq. to serve William Beverley of York River,

Virginia, lawyer.

William Harcum, baptised 29 December 1708, son of Thomas H., merchant tailor, admitted from St. Sepulchre; 16 July 1723 to his grandfather William Bryant and Mr. William Gerrish of London, merchant, to serve Nathaniel Webb Esq. of Montserrat.

Thomas Malcher, baptised 21 July 1706, son of Joseph M., framework knitter, admitted from St. Andrew Holborn; January 1721 to his mother Mrs. Jane Loe to serve Baptist Lasby of Antigua, merchant.

James Stock, baptised 20 January 1709, son of James S., joiner, admitted from St. Botolph Aldgate; 24 April 1723 to his mother Sarah S. and Mr. Thomas Trueman of London, merchant, to serve Joseph Hayton of Nevis, merchant.

William Bradford, baptised 29 March 1709, son of William B., cooper, admitted from St. Mildred Bread Street; 7 December 1726 to Stephen Proctor, Mr. of the *Cain Wood* bound for Barbados.

Edward Hill, born in November 1704, son of Richard H., feltmaker, admitted from St. Faith under St. Paul; 21 August 1718 to his sister Mary H. and Mr. Benjamin Bradley to serve John Allen of Virginia, merchant.

Wait Winthrop, baptised 6 May 1704, son of Jonathan W., mason, admitted from West Ham, Essex; 4 January 1718 to his said father to serve Dudley Woodbridge Esq. of Barbados.

William Wrighton, baptised 22 September 1706, son of John W., framework knitter, admitted from St. Leonard Shoreditch; 27 November 1721 to his sister Margaret Gambling and Edward Tyzack, mariner, to serve Rebecca Groves, widow, of Barbados.

John Wise, baptised 9 January 1707, son of John W., weaver, admitted from Stepney; 15 November 1721 by the consent of his ?aunt, Dorothy Paige, to serve Mr. John Pratt of Virginia, merchant.

William Trepas, baptised 16 December 1705, son of Thomas T., draper, admitted from St. Dunstan in the West; 27 February 1721 to his uncle Thomas Lee and John Tobin to serve Walter Tobin of Nevis, merchant.

Thomas Hedding, baptised 16 November 1706, son of John H., feltmaker, admitted from St. Martin in the Fields; 9 November 1720 to his aunt Letitia Hart to serve James Dickenson living in Maryland, mate of the *William & Hannah.*

John Terrill, baptised 28 December 1707, son of John T., carpenter, admitted from St. Mary Whitechapel; 11 November 1725 to his cousin Edward Scales to serve Stephen Pamflett, Mr. of the *Drewry & Elizabeth* bound for St. Christopher's.

William Dracot, baptised 2 January 1707, son of Richard D., tallow chandler, admitted from St. Botolph Bishopsgate; 20 September 1721 to Mr. Robert Man living in Chelsea to serve Mr. Edward Man of St. Christopher's, merchant.

John Smith, born 29 November 1709, son of Robert S., draper, admitted from St. Benet Paul's Wharf; 15 December 1726 to his friend John Keeley to serve John Jones, Mr. of the *Duke* bound for Maryland.

Thomas Grey, baptised 12 March 1707, son of William G., bowyer, admitted from Stepney; 31 May 1722 to his uncle William Marsland and Thomas Trueman, merchant, to serve Mr. Robert Pemberton of Nevis, merchant.

John Healy, baptised 18 December 1709, son of John H., fishmonger, admitted from St. Magnus the Martyr; 8 November 1723 to his friend Elizabeth Pollard to serve Arnold Livers of Potoxon River, Maryland.

Jacon Cawthorn, born 28 April 1705, son of Charles C., mason, admitted from St. Saviour Southwark; 8 November 1719 to his mother Phoebe C. and Micajah Perry Esq. to serve Charles Grimes of Virginia, merchant.

Thomas Beale, baptised 3 December 1702, son of Jonathan B., butcher, admitted from St. Clement Danes; 9 January 1719 to his mother Anne B. to serve Capt. Anthony Joad, Mr. of the *Midford* bound for Virginia.

William Dyer, baptised 15 October 1704, son of Edward D., plasterer, admitted from St. Andrew Holborn; 3 October 1720 to his cousin Mary D. to serve Robert Hanford, mate of the frigate *Troy* [or *Foy*] bound for Jamaica.

John Lukey, baptised 7 January 1707, son of Richard L., salter, admitted from St. Lawrence Old Jewry; 15 May 1725 to Richard Ryder, Mr. of the *Theodosia* trading to the West Indies.

Isaac Webb, baptised 4 June 1707, son of John W., feltmaker, admitted from St. Ann Blackfriars; 15 May 1725 to James Tregar, Mr. of the *Nancy* bound for the West Indies.

Thurston Adams, baptised 23 May 1703, son of John A., carpenter, admitted from St. Olave Silver Street; 24 November 1719 to his mother Jane A. and Davy Breholt, merchant, to serve Timothy Hare Esq. of St. Christopher's, merchant.

Thomas Yockkins, baptised 4 April 1706, son of Godfrey Y., plasterer, admitted from St. Bride's; 10 May 1720 to his said father and Mr. James Butler, merchant, to serve Mr. Robert Pemberton of Nevis, merchant.

Thomas Feering, born 24 March 1707, son of Thomas F., clothworker, admitted from St. Bartholomew the Less; 13 November 1725 to Thomas Sorrell, Mr. of the *Isabella & Mary* bound for Barbados.

William Crawley, baptised 16 April 1707, son of William C., tallow chandler, admitted from St. Dunstan Stepney; 14 August 1721 to his aunt Ann Taylor and William Tryon, merchant, to serve William Maidwell of St. Christopher's, merchant.

Thomas Davis, baptised 6 December 1707, son of Thomas D., armourer, admitted from Fulham, Middlesex; 12 January 1721 to his mother Elizabeth D. and Mr. John Berry, merchant, to serve Thomas Read of Virginia.

Peter Hudcoat, born 2 November 1707, son of Peter H., weaver, admitted from St. Benet Paul's Wharf; 3 August 1722 to his aunt Mary Redmayne and Mr. Joseph Macham, merchant, to serve James Field of Antigua, planter.

William Bosley, born 13 March 1707, son of James B., upholder, admitted from St. Peter Cornhill; 15 December 1721 to his mother Jane B. and Henry Chester of London, merchant, to serve Eyare Walcott of Barbados, attorney.

Edward Davy, born 28 August 1707, son of Edward D., merchant tailor, admitted from St. Mary Abchurch; 18 January 1723 to his mother Millicent D. and Mr. Henry Chester, merchant, to serve Sir William Coddrington for 3 years in England and 4 years in Antigua.

William Mills, born 20 January 1707, son of Robert M., weaver, admitted from St. Leonard Shoreditch; 24 April 1722 to his mother Jane M. to serve Mr. Christopher Stoodly of Antigua, merchant.

Joseph Bowes, born 17 June 1704, son of Ralph B., distiller, admitted from St. Giles Cripplegate; 12 December 1718 to his friend Mr. Henry Webster and Mr. Francis Melmoth, merchant, to serve Mr. James Knight of Kingston, Jamaica, merchant.

Marmaduke Holmes, baptised 21 October 1708, son of Christopher H., admitted from St. Dunstan in the East; 23 March 1724 to his said father and John Lloyd of London, merchant, to serve Andrew Faneuil of Boston, New England, merchant.

John Sheldon, born 21 January 1708, son of John S., admitted from St. James Clerkenwell in the place of Joseph Turner; 17 November 1722 to his mother Mary S. and Micajah Perry Esq. to serve Amos Garrett of Maryland, merchant.

Thomas Hardy, born 26 September 1708, son of John H., admitted from St. Saviour Southwark; 13 June 1724 to his friend Francis Warter and Mr. Thomas Barrow to serve Col. Parris, Secretary of Nevis.

Keilah Haswell, baptised 8 August 1706, son of John H., admitted from St. Martin Ludgate in the place of Ralph Rowland; 21 November 1722 to John Redman, Mr. of the frigate *Littleton* bound for the West Indies.

Robert Luddington, baptised 22 September 1707, son of Hugh L., skinner, admitted from St. Mary Whitechapel in the place of Mary Allen; 21 November 1724 to Abraham Lamb, Mr. of the galley *Betty* bound for Antigua.

William Gooding, baptised 30 August 1705, son of John G., embroiderer, admitted from St. James Clerkenwell in the place of James Mynds; 7 December 1719 to his said father and Micajah Perry Esq. to serve Phillip Ludwell Esq. of Virginia.

Admissions in April 1717

Mathew Brightridge, born 10 September 1709, son of Mathew B., clothworker, admitted from St. Sepulchre; 13 May 1727 to William Barfoot, Mr. of the *Radcliffe* bound for Jamaica.

William Lickorish, baptised 23 March 1707, son of William L., baker, admitted from St. Michael Bassishaw; 3 May 1721 to his father-in-law Thomas Fletcher and Micajah Perry Esq. to serve Robert Brooks Jr. of Rappahannock River, Virginia, merchant.

Thomas Clarke, baptised 15 May 1708, son of Thomas C., brewer, admitted from St. Giles Cripplegate; 7 May 1722 to his sister Elizabeth C. to serve Thomas Colmore, merchant living in St. Lawrence Pountney Lane, in Virginia.

Thomas Robins, born 11 August 1707, son of Thomas R., basket maker, admitted from St. Giles Cripplegate; 2 April 1722 to his said father and Mr. William Gerrish, merchant, to serve Mr. Joseph Simmons of Nevis, merchant.

Richard Blackford, baptised 3 April 1709, son of Richard B., joiner, admitted from St. Mary Rotherhithe, Surrey; 5 June 1724 to his cousin Richard B. to serve Francis Wells, Mr. of the galley *Hampstead* bound for New England.

Daniel Phillip Tuffery, baptised 8 October 1704, son of John T., admitted from St. James Westminster; 12 December 1719 to his mother Mary T. to serve Ephraim Langdon, Mr. of the *Hopewell* bound for Virginia.

William Fernall, baptised 30 October 1706, admitted from St. Mary at Hill; 23 January 1720 to his mother Elizabeth F. and Richard Coope, merchant, to serve Alexander Woodropp of St. Christopher's, merchant.

William Barlow, baptised 5 February 1710, son of Phillip B., horner, admitted from St. Ann Blackfriars; 4 May 1724 to his mother Mary B. to serve Nathaniel Cunningham of Boston, New England, merchant.

William Berrisford, baptised 20 February 1706, son of Julius B., wire drawer, admitted from St. Bartholomew the Less; 5 August 1721 to his aunt Elizabeth Fisher to serve Mr. Samuel Wadeson of Barbados, gent.

Thomas Science, baptised 11 April 1708, son of John S., stationer, admitted from St. Mary Somerset; 16 May 1723 to his mother Martha S. and Mr. Thomas Tryon gent. to serve John Tomlinson Esq. of Antigua, merchant.

John Cookes, born 22 September 1708, son of John C., mercer, admitted from St. Peter Cornhill; 16 May 1723 to his mother Johanna C. and Mr. Thomas Tryon gent. to serve Reynold Alleyne Esq. of Barbados.

John Butler, born 29 October 1708, son of John B., fruiterer, admitted from Stepney; 14 December 1722 to his mother Sarah Gascoigne [signs *Gaskell*] to serve Mrs. Mary Marshall of Spanish Town, Jamaica.

William Watson, baptised 17 December 1704, son of George W., harness maker, admitted from St. Andrew Holborn; 8 November 1719 to his mother Jane W. and Micajah Perry Esq. to serve Maj. Robert Bolling of Virginia, merchant.

Christopher Moe, baptised 17 November 1706, son of Thomas M., skinner, admitted from St. Ann Blackfriars in the place of Peter Bingham; 27 May 1720 to his mother Lettice M. and George Newport of London, merchant, to serve Hon. George Walker of Barbados, merchant.

William Lawne, born 6 January 1708, son of Mark L., fishmonger, admitted from St. James Westminster in the place of Thomas Merritt; October 1723 to his said father and Mr. Daniel Alford of London, merchant, to serve Tobias Wall of Nevis, merchant.

Admissions in April 1719

Alexander Strange, baptised 1 January 1713, son of William S., shipwright, admitted from St. Bride's; 17 December 1728 to Francis Rogers, Mr. of the *John & Judith* bound for Jamaica.

William Whitaker, born 23 July 1709, son of Edward W., admitted from St. Sepulchre; 10 September 1724 to his mother Sarah W. and John Rawlinson of Wood Street, dyer, to serve John Burke of Antigua, merchant.

Richard Knight, born 4 May 1710, son of Thomas K., stationer, admitted from St. Sepulchre; 13 November 1724 to his uncle Joseph Withall and Albert Nesbitt of London, merchant, to serve Francis Delap of Antigua, merchant.

William Carter, baptised 27 October 1710, son of Thomas C., carpenter, admitted from St. Giles Cripplegate; 13 July 1727 to his friend and guardian Mr. Simon Marshall to serve Joseph Richardson, Mr. of the *Frere* bound for Barbados.

John Tomlinson, born 1 April 1712, son of Samuel T., saddler, admitted from St. Ann Blackfriars; 3 March 1727 to his uncle Joseph T. and John Haddon Jr. to serve John Haddon Sr. in Antigua.

Paul Collier, baptised 14 April 1711, son of William C., stationer, admitted from St. Botolph Aldersgate; 29 May

1727 to his mother Mary Ann C. to serve John Ruggles living in Boston, New England, Mr. of the [blank] bound for Antigua.

John Powell, baptised 20 July 1707, son of Edmond P., stationer, admitted from St. Ann Blackfriars; 13 November 1725 to William Carry, Mr. of the *Thetis* bound for the West Indies.

James Lane, baptised 13 July 1710, son of John L., clothworker, admitted from St. Botolph Bishopsgate; 8 December 1724 to his mother Elizabeth L. to serve Michael Lynch of Montserrat, merchant.

Edward Wilson, baptised 13 August 1711, son of Robert W., admitted from St. Dunstan in the East in the place of Samuel Mitchell; 3 August 1726 to his mother Ann W. to serve Nathaniel Lloyd of Jamaica, merchant.

John Legg, baptised 26 July 1709, son of Richard L., barber surgeon, admitted by special order of Court; 3 August 1722 to his mother Mary L. and Mr. Joseph Adams of Mincing Lane, merchant, to serve Col. Jacob Morgan of Antigua, merchant.

Joseph Russell, born 28 November 1712, son of Joseph R., admitted from St. Stephen Coleman Street in the place of William Kemp; 17 December 1728 to Thomas Bell, Mr. of the *Mary* bound for Barbados.

William Tampion, baptised 27 April 1712, son of John T., admitted from All Hallows Barking in the place of Alexander Goodall; 27 May 1725 to his brother-in-law Samuel Bantoft and Henry Chester, merchant, to serve Sir William Coddrington in Antigua.

John Smith, born 23 January 1711, son of Thomas S., haberdasher, admitted from St. Giles Cripplegate in the place of James Castle; 13 November 1727 to his mother Martha S. to serve Francis Rogers, Mr. of the *John & Judith* bound for Jamaica.

Admissions in April 1721

Thomas Rose, baptised 28 March 1718, son of John R., upholder, admitted from St. Mary le Strand; 10 March 1728 to his mother Ann R. and Mr. Robert Hume, apothecary in Southwark, to serve Peter Hume of London Town, Maryland.

Maynard Kingsley, born 12 July 1710, son of Richard K., carpenter, admitted from St. Dunstan in the East; 13 September 1725 to his mother Ruth K. and Mary Phenney to serve her husband George Phenney Esq., Governor of the Bahamas.

John Cue, born 15 July 1714, son of John C., draper, admitted from St. John Hackney, Middlesex; 1 April 1729 to his aunt Jane Pinfold and Mr. Slingsby Bethell, merchant, to serve George Lucas of Antigua, merchant.

Francis Hooker, born 28 November 1707, son of George H., weaver, admitted from St. Giles Cripplegate; 26 July 1723 to Mr. Daniel Alford, merchant, to serve Richard Hankshaw of St. Christopher's, merchant.

Charles Howson, born 22 March 1712, son of John H., butcher, admitted from St. Mary Whitechapel; 28 September 1727 to his aunt Margaret Hawkins to serve Samuel Ashurst of London, merchant, in Jamaica.

John Jones, baptised 26 August 1710, son of James J., joiner, admitted from St. Botolph Aldgate; 15 January 1725 to his mother Mary J. and Nathaniel Barnardiston, merchant, to serve Col. John Davie of St. Christopher's, merchant.

James Alport, baptised 27 September 1712, son of James A., draper, admitted from St. Benet Fink; 28 March 1728 to his uncle James Careless living at Whitechapel Church and Mr. George Strode of London, merchant, to serve Hon. Timothy Salter of Barbados, merchant.

Robert Fox, baptised 1 June 1712, son of William F., gunmaker, admitted from St. Botolph Aldgate; 29 December 1727 to his said father and Crooke Thomas of Crutched Friars, merchant, to serve Josiah Martin of Antigua, merchant.

Robert Cambridge, baptised 10 February 1713, son of John C., pewterer, admitted from St. Mary Whitechapel; 15 April 1728 to his guardian Mr. Thomas Mason and Micajah Perry Esq. to serve Richard Bennett Esq. of Maryland, merchant.

John Denton, baptised 26 September 1713, son of Richard D., blacksmith, admitted from St. Mary le Bow; 3 November 1731 to Arthur Payne, Mr. of the *Antigua Merchant* bound for Antigua.

William Buck, baptised 13 September 1713, son of Thomas B., barber surgeon, admitted from Enfield, Middlesex; 10 September 1728 to his uncle William Howell to serve Col. William Randolph of James River, Virginia, merchant.

William Raw, born 30 December 1712, son of Adam R., barber surgeon, admitted from St. Margaret Lothbury; 21 January 1730 to his mother Sarah Achurch to serve William Bryant, Mr. of the *Alderly* bound for New York.

Samuel Norton, baptised 11 January 1714, son of Charles N., weaver, admitted from St. Dunstan Stepney; 14 June 1729 to William Lea, Mr. of the *Carolina Regina* bound for Holland and Pennsylvania.

William Baker, born 10 September 1713, son of Joseph B., tallow chandler, admitted from St. Sepulchre; 15 November 1729 to Robert Clark, Mr. of the *Crowley* bound for Jamaica.

Richard Crowley, baptised 4 February 1713, son of William C., admitted from St. Katherine Creechurch in the place of William Hertford; 18 November 1728 by the consent of his mother Levinia Mearea and uncle William Hughes to serve Mr. James Douglass of London, merchant, in Antigua.

Thomas Lane, baptised 16 January 1709, son of Noel L., admitted from St. Katherine Creechurch in the place of George Oxnard; 7 May 1724 to his grandmother Susanna L. to serve John Caswell of London, merchant, or his brother Henry Caswell of Boston, New England, merchant.

Admissions in April 1722

John Shickle, born in May 1713, son of Edward S., skinner, admitted from St. Mary Whitechapel; 8 March 1728 to his brother Thomas S. and Mr. George Auchterlony of London, merchant, to serve Messrs Fearand Dawkins and Malcomb of Jamaica, merchants.

William Bacchus, born 12 March 1713, son of Richard B., blacksmith, admitted from St. Dunstan in the West; 31 January 1728 to his mother Jane Burton and Henry Chester, merchant, to serve Edward Chester Jr. of Antigua, merchant.

Edward Barber, baptised 12 December 1714, son of Edward B., butcher, admitted from St. Botolph Bishopsgate; 30 April 1729 to his said father and Mr. Thomas Corbett, sugar baker, to serve Thomas Davers of Barbados, planter.

John Fisher, baptised 14 June 1713, son of Joseph F., vintner, admitted from St. Andrew Holborn; 6 September 1728 to his said farther and Mr. James Douglas of London, merchant, to serve Mr. Thomas Fenton of Antigua, merchant.

Thomas Black, baptised 15 February 1714, son of James B., barber surgeon, admitted from St. Dunstan Stepney; 3 November 1731 to Ambrose Cock, Mr. of the *Monmouth* bound for Maryland.

John Hill, baptised 13 August 1713, son of Henry H., weaver, admitted from St. Botolph Bishopsgate; 5 August 1728 to his mother Mary H. and James Douglass, merchant, to serve [blank] of Antigua, merchant.

Henry Reeve, baptised 26 September 1711, son of Henry R., goldsmith, admitted from St. Edmund the King; 1 December 1729 to his mother Thomasin R. to serve Thomas Cull, Mr. of the *Friends Adventure* bound for Nevis.

Samuel Daniel, born in June 1711, son of Samuel D., weaver, admitted from St. Mary Whitechapel; 2 March 1726 to his uncle Samuel Walley [signs *Richard Whaley*], apothecary of Snow Hill, to serve George Hall of Port Royal, Jamaica.

John Withers, baptised 6 September 1713, son of William W., salter, admitted from Wandsworth, Surrey; 19 January 1728 by the consent of his uncle William Clarke to Mr. John Caswell, merchant, to serve John Yeamans of Antigua, merchant.

Christopher Goddard, born 10 May 1714, son of Benjamin G., clockmaker, admitted from St. Giles Cripplegate; 26 March 1731 to his uncle James G. to serve William Bryant, Mr. of the *Albany* bound for New York.

Thomas Mapleston, born 20 September 1712, son of James M., weaver, admitted from St. Dunstan Stepney; 17 December 1728 to Richard Crookenden, Mr. of the *Harbin* bound for Barbados.

Samuel Waterman, baptised 30 September 1711, son of Lawrence W., bricklayer, admitted from St. Lawrence Jewry; 22 April 17— to his mother Priscilla W. and Samuel Wragg, merchant, to serve John Wright and Gibson Clapp of South Carolina, merchants.

John Martin, baptised in March 1715, son of John M., saddler, admitted from St. Giles in the Fields; 9 March 1731 to his sister Christian M. to serve Thomas Smith, Mr. of the *Beaver* bound for New York.

Alexander Bryers, baptised 31 March 1713, son of William B., cooper, admitted from St. Botolph Aldgate; 3 October 1728 to his uncle Thomas B. and Mr. Philip Perry on behalf of his brother Micajah Perry, merchant, to serve Capt. Wilson Cary of Hampton, Virginia.

Edward Allen, baptised 11 July 2724, son of John A., tiler and bricklayer, admitted from St. Botolph Bishopsgate; 15 May 1731 to Edward How, Mr. of the *Lady Amelia* bound for Jamaica.

Samuel Howlett, baptised 29 January 1712, son of Nicholas H., vintner, admitted from St. Giles in the Fields; 5 September 1726 to his uncle John Passmore to serve Joshua Gabourel, Mr. of the *Maxwell* bound for Barbados.

John Hutton, born 26 April 1715, son of John H., loriner, admitted from St. Sepulchre; 26 December 1730 to his mother Sarah Crofts and Mr. Eliakim Palmer of London, merchant, to serve John Ashley Esq. of Barbados, merchant.

Henry Peete, baptised 24 January 1710, son of Richard P., leatherseller, admitted from St. Mary Whitechapel; 23 February 1725 to his mother Margaret P. and Joseph Haden of Wapping, sailmaker, to serve his son Joseph Haden of Boston, New England.

William West, baptised 15 June 1713, son of George W., spectacle maker, admitted from St. Olave Southwark; 17 September 1728 to his mother Jane W. and Joseph Gerrish of London, merchant, to serve Michael Lynch of Montserrat, merchant.

Thomas Edwards, born 12 June 1723, son of Thomas E., feltmaker, admitted from St. Olave Southwark; 4 July 1726 to his said father to serve John Fawson and Robert Munday of Kingston, Jamaica, merchants.

Henry Smith, baptised 29 November 1710, son of Anthony S., admitted from St. Leonard Shoreditch in the place of Henry Everett; 17 December 1724 to his brother Anthony S. to serve John Gregory of Jamaica, gent.

William Mathews, born 4 March 1712, son of Samuel M., admitted from St. Bride's in the place of Thomas Barlow; 21 December 1728 to William Overall, Mr. of the galley *Eaton* bound for Jamaica.

Daniel Hamblin, baptised in 1714, son of Samuel H. of Sherborne, Dorset, admitted in the place of Shaulet King; 15 December 17— to his friend Henry Sheppard and Mr. Peter Delamotte of London, merchant, to serve James

Fallon of St. Christopher's, merchant.

Admissions in April 1723

Thomas Barker Knowles, born 6 January 1715, son of John K., carpenter, admitted from St. Giles in the Fields; 7 January 1730 to his mother Mary K. to serve Mr. Amos Woodward of Annapolis, Maryland, merchant.

William Nicholson, born 16 December 1712, son of William N., leatherseller, admitted from St. Mary Magdalene Bermondsey, Surrey; 12 May 1727 to his great aunt Jane, wife of Richard Brown of Barnaby Street, and his uncle Thomas Matthews and Samuel Wragg, merchant, to serve John Lynch of Jamaica, merchant.

Robert Knighton, born 18 August 1713, son of Thomas K., joiner, admitted from St. Botolph Bishopsgate; 24 May 1728 by the consent of his relation Mr. Charles Carkesse to serve Archibald Cochran of Antigua, merchant.

William Quilter, baptised 12 August 1714, son of John Q., butcher, admitted from St. Leonard Eastcheap; 12 November 1728 to his aunt Catherine Smith to serve Archibald Esdaile of St. Christopher's, merchant.

William Knight, baptised 21 February 1714, son of Joseph K., cooper, admitted from St. James Garlickhithe; 1 April 1729 to his mother Lucy K. and Slingsby Bethell, merchant, to serve Nathaniel Crump of Antigua, merchant.

Thomas Wint, baptised 4 December 1715, son of Samuel W., joiner, admitted from St. Margaret Westminster; 27 November 1730 to his said father and George Auchterlony of London, merchant, to serve Messrs. Fearon and Malcolm of Jamaica, merchants.

Samuel Martin, baptised 13 November 1715, son of Samuel M., weaver, admitted from St. Mary Whitechapel; 16 October 1730 to his mother Elizabeth M. and Mr. Jonathan Gale of London, merchant of Bush Lane, Cannon Street, to serve Mr. Isaac Gale of St. Elizabeth's parish, Jamaica, merchant.

Richard Hacker, baptised 1 March 1713, son of John H., tinplate worker, admitted from All Hallows Barking; 24 May 1728 to his mother Ann H. and Roland Fry of London, merchant, to serve George Byam of Antigua, merchant.

William Gurney, born 18 January 1714, son of William G., feltmaker, admitted from St. Leonard Shoreditch; 26 October 1728 to his mother Ann G. and Micajah Perry Esq. to serve [blank].

John Page, born 24 September 1715, son of Robert P., merchant tailor, admitted from St. Giles Cripplegate; 3 November 1731 to Benjamin Cowell, Mr. of the *Shelbourne* bound for Jamaica.

Thomas Simmons, baptised 16 June 1714, son of Michael S., currier, admitted from St. Andrew Holborn; 2 April 1729 to his uncle Samuel Wheeler and Slingsby Bethell, merchant, to serve Nathaniel Gilbert of Antigua, merchant.

Thomas Williams, born 11 November 1713, son of Thomas W., salter, admitted from St. Mary Magdalen Bermondsey, Surrey; October 1726 to his said father and Mr. Humphrey Hill of Broad Street to serve Mr. John Burke of Antigua, merchant.

Henry Bayley, born 12 February 1714, son of Thomas B., pewterer, admitted from St. Sepulchre; 28 December 1728 to his uncle Henry Brumwell and Mr. Edwin Somers, merchant, to serve Hon. John Colleton of Barbados, merchant.

Richard Luffe, baptised 8 January 1716, son of Richard L., admitted from St. Giles Cripplegate in the place of Richard Rogers deceased; January 1731 to his friend Mr. Thomas Bridges to serve Mr. John Caswell of London, merchant, in London or Boston, New England.

Samuel Ferriman, baptised 13 February 1715, son of John F., fishmonger, admitted from Christ Church in the place of Robert Blackwell; 22 July 1729 to his mother Hannah F.

and John Serocold of London, merchant, to serve Thomas Halse Esq. of Jamaica, planter.

Samuel Arnold, baptised 1 April 1716, son of John A., admitted from St. Dunstan in the East; 22 July 1731 to his mother Elizabeth A. and Mr. Ralph Noden, merchant, to serve Mr. Henry Corbusier of Bermuda, merchant.

Admissions in April 1724

Nathaniel Morris Patteson, baptised 28 December 1717, son of Nathaniel P., barber surgeon, admitted from St. Lawrence Jewry; 20 June 1733 to his said father and Mr. Rowland Frye of Great Tower Street to serve Mr. John Frye Jr. of Antigua.

James Smith, baptised 10 February 1715, son of William S., stationer, admitted from St. Paul Shadwell; 11 November 1729 to his mother Jane S. and Thomas Beckford of London, merchant, to serve Peter Beckford and Edward Grant Esqs. of Jamaica.

John Gardner, born 14 February 1713, son of John G., goldsmith, admitted from St. Giles Cripplegate; 26 January 1728 to his said father and Henry Chester, merchant, to serve Edward Chester Jr., merchant, in Antigua.

Daniel Rigneere Thomas, son of Robert T., cordwainer, admitted from St. Thomas Southwark; 3 July 1733 to his mother Ann Moore and Thomas Beckford Esq. to serve William Whitehorn of St. Ann's, Jamaica, merchant.

John Lindsey, baptised 6 March 1716, son of John L., merchant tailor, admitted from St. Dunstan in the West; 11 November 1729 to his said father and Thomas Beckford, merchant, to serve Peter Beckford and Edward Grant of Jamaica, merchants.

George Ginn, born 1 April 1716, son of William G., feltmaker, admitted from St. Bartholomew the Less; 17 August 1730 to his cousin Anna Maria Harding to serve Thomas Butler of London, merchant, in Nevis.

Thomas Harward, born 24 October 1717, son of John H., barber surgeon, admitted from All Hallows Lombard Street; —— 1733 by the consent of his mother Elinor H. and Slingsby Bethell, merchant, to serve [blank] of Antigua, merchant.

James Smart, born 6 September 1716, son of Isaac S., loriner, admitted from St. Sepulchre; 21 October 1732 to Edward Phillips, Mr. of the frigate *Constant* bound for Jamaica.

Edward Bryan, baptised 3 September 1711, son of John B., haberdasher, admitted from St. Ann Blackfriars; 21 July 1726 to his mother Margaret B. and Mr. William Coleman, merchant, to serve Drewry Ottley Esq. of St. Christopher's, merchant.

James Jackson, baptised 28 April 1716, son of Samuel J., barber surgeon, admitted from St. John the Baptist; 9 December 1730 to Thomas Tryon, merchant, to serve Jasper Verchild of St. Christopher's, planter.

William Walmsley, born 3 November 1715, son of William W., cordwainer, admitted from St. Giles Cripplegate; 8 May 17— by the consent of his uncle Thomas W. to serve Robert Paramore living in Boston, New England, Mr. of the *Almsbury*.

Charles Abbott, born 9 June 1717, son of William A., salter, admitted from St. Michael Royal; 14 March 1732 to his said father to serve Mr. William Crawford of London, mariner, in Jamaica.

Timothy Tweedy, baptised 16 December 1716, son of James T., stationer, admitted from St. Swithin's; 5 February 1732 to his said father to serve John Ayscough Esq. in Jamaica.

Thomas Brown, baptised 13 December 1714, son of Thomas B., merchant tailor, admitted from St. Clement Danes; 18 March 1729 to his uncle Robert Scrooby and John Midford, merchant of Mincing Lane, to serve Benjamin Tasker Esq., Naval Officer of Annapolis, Maryland.

George Seaton, baptised 7 May 1716, son of George S.,

merchant tailor, admitted from St. Anne and St. Agnes; 3 June 1731 to his said father and Mr. John Serocold, merchant, to serve Maj. Richard Newsum of Jamaica, planter.

Joseph Woodyatt, baptised 23 November 1716, son of Edward W., hatband maker, admitted from St. Vedast; 7 September 1732 to his said father and Mr. Thomas Butler of Camberwell, merchant, to serve Col. John Williams of Antigua, merchant.

James Mullens, baptised 10 February 1717, son of William M., barber surgeon, admitted from St. Lawrence Jewry; 31 October 1733 to Robert Clarke, Mr. of the *Crowley* bound for Jamaica.

Matthew Munt, baptised 2 March 1718, son of Isaac M., joiner, admitted from St. Helen's; 10 March 1733 to his said father and Roger Drake of London, merchant, to serve Richard Drake of Jamaica, merchant.

Josias Harper, born 12 November 1713, son of Henry H., poulterer, admitted from St. Mary Magdalene Bermondsey, Surrey; October 1728 to his mother Mary H. and Thomas Beckford, merchant, to serve Peter Beckford of Jamaica, merchant.

Robert Barrett, baptised 21 July 1716, son of John B., admitted from Thetford, Norfolk, by special order of Court; 14 January 17— to his friend Rev. Peter Selby and John Serocold, merchant, to serve Richard Hemings Esq. of St. Ann's, Jamaica.

James Cox, born 22 July 1713, son of James C., fishmonger, admitted from St. Michael Queenhithe in the place of William Lee; 30 August 1728 to his sister Sarah C. and Thomas Tryon, merchant, to serve Mrs. Elizabeth Alleyne, widow, in Barbados.

Admissions in April 1725

Thomas Dove, baptised 7 July 1715, son of Thomas D.,

merchant tailor, admitted from St. John Wapping; 9 October 1731 to Thomas Dove, Mr. of the *Bailey* bound for Virginia.

John Cobb, baptised 26 October 1716, son of John C., weaver, admitted from St. Dunstan Stepney; 27 July 1732 to his mother Martha C. and Mr. Thomas Parsons, merchant, to serve Capt. Samuel Spofforth of Bermuda, merchant.

Peter Beauchamp, baptised 13 March 1719, son of John B., fishmonger, admitted from St. Edmund the King; 22 October 1735 to John Sutton, Mr. of the *Fane* bound for St. Christopher's.

Richard Shann, baptised 8 November 1715, son of William S., plasterer, admitted from St. Stephen Coleman Street; 2 January 1731 to his sister Ann S. to serve Mr. John Grove, merchant, in Barbados.

Thomas Atwell, baptised 3 February 1717, son of William A., blacksmith, admitted from St. Benet Paul's Wharf; 28 July 1731 to his mother Mary Horton and Thomas Strode, merchant, to serve Richard Salter Esq. of Barbados.

Thomas Pearce, born 24 January 1716, son of Phillip P., weaver, admitted from St. Giles Cripplegate; 14 February 1730 to his mother Mary P. and Slingsby Bethell, merchant, to serve John Duer Esq. of Antigua.

Thomas Wondey, born 27 March 1718, son of Thomas W., painter stainer, admitted from St. Botolph Bishopsgate; 8 September 1733 to his said father and Mr. Eliakim Palmer, merchant, to serve Thomas Leake and Thomas Cheesman, merchants, in Barbados

John Clements, born 2 December 1715, son of John C., coachmaker, admitted from St. Martin in the Fields; 12 September 1730 to his uncle Thomas Stedman to serve Theophilus Gregory of St. George the Martyr, Middlesex, in Carolina and to learn the art of merchandizing.

Robert Sharp, baptised 16 July 1715, son of Robert S., weaver, admitted from St. Botolph Bishopsgate; 15 December 1730

to his grandmother Elizabeth Tarrant and James Buchanan of London, merchant, to serve Col. John Syme of Hanover Co., Virginia, surveyor and merchant.

John Hopkins, born 13 April 1713, son of John H., blacksmith, admitted from St. Stephen Coleman Street; 13 December 1728 to his uncle Richard Haynes and William Coleman, merchant, to serve Penelope Mead of St. Christopher's, merchant.

William Swift, born 22 August 1715, son of John S., clothworker, admitted from St. Mary Magdalene Bermondsey, Surrey; 13 May 1730 to his said father and Thomas Butler, merchant, to serve Col. William Pym of St. Christopher's, planter.

Thomas Bond, baptised in June 1716, son of Christopher B., founder, admitted from St. Dunstan Stepney; 20 October 1731 to his mother Mary Silvester and Mr. Roger Drake, merchant, to serve Henry Dawkins Esq. of Jamaica.

Newman Hayes, baptised 24 July 1716, son of William H., joiner, admitted from St. Mary Whitechapel; 26 January 1732 to his said father to serve Richard Lee of Potuxon River, Maryland, merchant.

Christopher Sutton, born 5 June 1715, son of Christopher S., cooper, admitted from St. John Wapping; 17 February 1730 to his mother Ann S. and Thomas Trueman, merchant, to serve Charles Payne of St. Christopher's, planter.

Robert Helbye, born 14 July 1716, son of John H., joiner, admitted from St. Bride's; 29 July 1729 to his uncle Richard Sizer and John Serocold, merchant, to serve Thomas Halse Esq. of Jamaica, planter.

John Cox, born 9 December 1715, son of John C., merchant tailor, admitted from St. Botolph Bishopsgate; 21 March 1730 to his said father and John Caswell, merchant, to serve Col. Samuel Brown of New England, merchant.

William Simpson, born 21 April 1717, son of John S., weaver, admitted from St. Botolph Aldersgate; 26 February 1732 to his said father and William Tryon, merchant, to serve Aston Warner, Attorney-General of Antigua.

Thomas Parker, baptised 27 December 1717, son of Edward P., joiner, admitted from St. Giles Cripplegate; 29 July 1734 with the consent of Elizabeth P. to Thomas Henning of Charles Town, South Carolina, Mr. of the *Success* bound for the West Indies.

Isaac Hubbald, baptised 7 June 1719, son of Isaac H., haberdasher, admitted from St. Mary Rotherhithe, Surrey; 11 February 1734 to his aunt Mary Clark and Margaret Santanca to serve her husband Thomas S., surgeon apothecary of Clarendine Mount, Jamaica.

Abraham Walker, baptised 26 October 1718, son of George W., butcher, admitted from St. Ethelburga; 16 January 1733 to his mother Mary W. and Mr. Henry Lascelles of London, merchant of Mincing Lane, to serve Hon. John Frere of Barbados, planter.

James Mills, baptised 31 May 1717, son of Robert M., weaver, admitted from St. Leonard Shoreditch; 28 July 1733 to his mother Sarah M. and John Myres to serve William Hinton, Mr. of the *Frant* bound for St. Christopher's.

Thomas Vernon, baptised 28 December 1715, son of Francis V., joiner, admitted from Richmond, Surrey; 6 December 1729 to his mother Margaret V. and Thomas Tryon, merchant, to serve Thomas Dotin Esq. of Barbados.

Thomas Coningsby, born in August 1718, son of Thomas C., haberdasher, admitted from St. Alphage; 27 October 1732 to his mother Sarah C. and Slingsby Bethell, merchant, to serve John Wickham of Antigua, merchant.

George Whitlock, baptised 12 April 1716, son of James W., clockmaker, admitted from St. Sepulchre; 16 August 1731 to his friend Mr. Thomas Allcraft to serve Phillip Dummer Esq. of Boston, New England.

Edward Perry, born in May 1717, son of John P., butcher, admitted from St. Botolph Bishopsgate; 13 October 1732 to his aunt Susanna Bangough and Joseph Cobb, mariner, to serve William Cunningham of Jamaica, merchant.

John Baynes, baptised 3 October 1714, son of John B., merchant tailor, admitted from St. Peter le Poor; 13 April 1731 with the consent of his mother Johanna B. to Tobias Wall of London, merchant, to serve Nicholas Gollway of St. Christopher's, merchant.

Dickinson Vincent, baptised 4 November 1719, son of Richard V., goldsmith, admitted from St. Ann Aldersgate; 22 October 1735 to James Belcher, Mr. of the *Timothy & Jacob* bound for York River, Virginia.

John Webster, baptised 29 June 1718, son of John W., carman, admitted from St. Botolph Aldersgate; 22 October 1735 to John Davison, Mr. of the *Britannia* bound for Jamaica.

John Burr, baptised 17 February 1721, son of George B., turner, admitted from St. James Westminster; 6 April 1736 to his brother William B. and Mr. John Rogers to serve Sir William Coddrington in Antigua.

Joshua Pussey, born in February 1715, son of John P., joiner, admitted from St. John the Baptist in the place of Thomas Abbison; 18 February 1730 to his aunt Frances Mindham and Thomas Butler of London, merchant, to serve Thomas Stevens, merchant in Antigua.

Joseph Boardman, baptised 13 February 1717, son of Robert B., pewterer, admitted from St. Dunstan in the East; 21 August 1731 to his mother Amey B. and Mr. John Elton of St. Margaret Westminster to serve Mr. Francis Wells of Boston, New England, merchant.

William Taylor, baptised 31 January 1714, son of William T., glazier, admitted from Fulham, Middlesex; 25 February 1729 to his mother Ann Bennett and Thomas Lane on behalf of Mr. John Caswell, merchant, to serve Henry Lane of New York, merchant.

John Zigenhorn, baptised 28 September 1716, son of John Joseph Z., admitted from St. John Wapping; 2 October 1734 to Robert ?Wheatle, Mr. of the *Bonetta* bound for Jamaica.

Jonathan Turner, baptised 8 June 1718, son of Jonathan T., admitted from [blank]; 28 September 1733 to his mother Elizabeth T. and Eliakim Palmer of Aldermanbury, merchant, to serve John Ashley Esq. of Barbados, merchant.

Admissions in April 1727

Griffin Wright, baptised 12 February 1719, son of Griffin W., fruiterer, admitted from St. Martin Vintry; 18 January 1733 to his uncle John Waite and Daniel Lamport, merchant of Oxford Court, London, to serve Col. George Braxton of York River, Virginia, merchant.

William Willson, baptised 12 June 1720, son of Benjamin W., joiner, admitted from St. James Clerkenwell; 9 June 1736 to John Nickelson, Mr. of the *Pelham* bound for South Carolina.

John Fowkes, baptised 24 August 1715, son of Ellis F., butcher, admitted from Christ Church; 26 November 1732 to his mother Mary F. and George Ochterlony, merchant, to serve Messrs. Fearon and Malcolm of Jamaica, merchants.

Solomon Heathcote, baptised 9 February 1721, son of William H., shipwright, admitted from St. Mary at Hill; 6 December 1736 to his friend William Mingay of Gracechurch Street and Mr. John Maynard Jr. of London, merchant, to serve John Clayton Esq., Attorney-General of Virginia.

John Still, baptised 5 July 1716, son of John S., basketmaker, admitted from St. Botolph Aldersgate; 9 December 1730 to his mother Sarah S. and Thomas Tryon of London, merchant, to serve Thomas Dotin of Barbados, planter.

John Ellard, baptised 11 August 1717, son of Edward E., feltmaker, admitted from St. Giles Cripplegate; 4 August 1732 to his mother Mary E. to serve Humphrey Bell of

London, merchant, in Virginia or Maryland.

John Coolidge, born 18 January 1718, son of John C., shipwright, admitted from St. Paul Shadwell; 27 October 1733 to Thomas Shubrick, Mr. of the *Mary Ann* bound for South Carolina.

Thomas Kynaston, baptised 16 March 1718, son of Thomas K., poulterer, admitted from Christ Church; 27 March 1734 to his said father and Mr. Henry Lascelles of London, merchant, to serve Robert Allen of Barbados, planter.

Admissions in April 1728

Jacob Wright, baptised 12 April 1719, son of William W., merchant tailor, admitted from St. Mary Abchurch; 14 June 1734 to his mother Mary Jepps to serve Edward Jones of Bermuda, merchant.

William Empson, baptised 13 August 1720, son of John E., carpenter, admitted from All Hallows London Wall; 17 February 1735 to his mother Winifred E. and Thomas Phillips of Boston, New England, merchant, to serve Abraham Winder of Boston, ship chandler.

James Martin, baptised 22 September 1719, son of Robert M., barber surgeon, admitted from St. Giles in the Fields; 12 February 1734 to his mother Sarah M. and Beeston Long of London, merchant, to serve Hon. Edward Pennant Esq. of Clarendon, Jamaica, merchant.

Charles Milton, baptised 29 September 1720, son of Francis M., leatherseller, admitted from Greenwich, Kent; 22 October 1735 with the consent of his mother Hester M. to Mr. Roger Drake of London, merchant, to serve John Pennant of Clarendon, Jamaica, merchant.

Michael Gurnell, baptised 13 November 1718, son of Mantle G., weaver, admitted from St. Botolph Aldgate; 9 January 1733 to his uncle Michael G. and Mr. Henry Lascelles of Mincing Lane, merchant, to serve Hon. John Frere of Barbados, planter.

Francis Richards, baptised 25 December 1716, son of Jonathan R., mason, admitted from Greenwich, Kent; 29 March 1732 to his mother Ann R. and Roger Drake of London, merchant, to serve Henry Barham Esq. of Jamaica.

Roger Bow, baptised 28 July 1721, son of Roger B., waterman, admitted from Putney, Surrey; 23 October 1736 to Matthias Job Bankes, Mr. of the *Beckford* bound for the West Indies.

John West, baptised 28 February 1720, son of John W., bricklayer, admitted from Holy Trinity Minories; 25 February 1735 to his aunt Mary Harbin to serve Mr. Peter Vanbrugh Livingston of New York, merchant.

James Peacock, baptised 14 October 1718, son of William P., cordwainer, admitted from St. Botolph Bishopsgate; 20 June 1733 to his mother Mary Newton and Mr. Rowland Frye of Great Tower Street to serve Mr. Francis Delap of Antigua, merchant.

William Clark, baptised 30 January 1724, son of Joseph C., carpenter, admitted from St. Thomas Southwark; 15 December 1738 to his uncle Henry Ashbey and Daniel Lascelles of London, merchant, to serve John Frere of Barbados, planter.

John Hellier, baptised 12 July 1720, son of John H., admitted from Sherborne, Dorset, in the place of Esau Gent; 23 September 1735 to his aunt Ann Kemp and Mr. Roger Drake of London, merchant, to serve Henry Barham of Jamaica, planter.

Richard Dracott, baptised 2 August 1720, son of Timothy D., admitted from Newbury, Berkshire; 21 October 1735 to his aunt Jane Wilson to serve Florentius Vassell of Fenchurch Street Buildings in Jamaica.

Admissions in April 1729

Joshua Cock, baptised 8 October 1722, son of James C., haberdasher, admitted from St. Botolph Bishopsgate;

21 October 1737 to his friend Charles Dodsworth and Mr. David Currie of London, merchant, to serve Florentius Vassell of Jamaica, merchant.

Joseph Wibird, baptised 25 June 1718, son of John W., leatherseller, admitted from St. Ethelburga; 9 November 1733 to his mother Mary Robsin and Samuel Salmon of Barbados, merchant, to serve Elizabeth Shaw of Bridgetown, Barbados.

Peter Hopkins, born in November 1720, son of John H., cooper, admitted from St. Sepulchre; 17 December 1736 to his father-in-law John Foster and Thomas Strode of London, merchant, to serve Jonathan Blenman of Barbados to learn the art of book-keeping.

Paul Hoare, baptised 25 January 1720, son of George H., butcher, admitted from St. Botolph Aldgate; 5 May 1736 to his said father and Mr. Tobias Wall of London, merchant, to serve John Anderson of St. Christopher's, merchant.

Thomas Everard, baptised 16 August 1719, son of William E., skinner, admitted from St. Paul Shadwell; 10 January 1735 to his uncle Edward E. and Edward Athawes, merchant of King Court, Lombard Street, to serve Matthew Kemp of Williamsburgh, Virginia, merchant.

Roberts Akers, baptised 16 December 1719, son of John A., poulterer, admitted from Christ Church; 5 June 1736 to Edmond Smyter, Mr. of the *Mercury* bound for America.

Admissions in April 1730

Thomas Perkins, baptised 27 January 1720, son of Richard P., girdler, admitted from St. Katherine Creechurch; 17 October 1735 to his cousin Mr. Henry Hall and Mr. John Maynard of Great St. Helen's, merchant, to serve John Clayton Jr., Clerk of Gloucester County, Virginia.

James Booth, baptised 22 February 1719, son of Francis B., joiner, admitted from St. Mary Magdalen Old Fish Street; 25 October 1735 to William Mason, Mr. of the *Morrice* bound for Jamaica.

Edmund Robinson, born in December 1722, son of James R., turner, admitted from St. Giles Cripplegate; 1 June 1738 to his mother Ann R. to serve John Beard, Mr. of the *Charming Molly* bound for the West Indies.

Daniel Swinorton, baptised 19 June 1720, son of James S., barber surgeon, admitted from St. George the Martyr, Southwark; 15 August 1735 to his uncle John Langworthy and Mr. John Caswell of New England, merchant, to serve Henry Caswell of Boston, New England.

Nathaniel John Cooper, baptised 11 January 1719, son of [blank], haberdasher, admitted from St. Sepulchre; 23 October 1736 to Thomas Walker, Mr. of the *John & Mary* bound for Madeira and Barbados.

Charles Weale, baptised 6 June 1722, son of Charles W., haberdasher, admitted from St. Bride's; 16 July 1737 to his said father and Thomas Lane of Nicholas Lane, merchant, to serve Peter Faneuil Esq. of Boston, New England, merchant.

William Salter, baptised 1 January 1721, son of Thomas S., turner, admitted from St. Sepulchre; 19 October 1734 to his mother Sarah S. and Mr. Thomas Bolling, Mr. of the *Essex*, to serve Col. Lewis Burwell of James River, Virginia, merchant.

David Baschard, baptised 18 September 1720, son of David B., mason, admitted from St. Vedast; 15 February 1735 to his mother Mary B. to serve Thomas Phillips of Boston, New England, merchant.

Robert Man, baptised in June 1722, son of Edmund M., admitted from St. Martin in the Fields; 22 May 1736 to Humphrey Conway, Mr. of the *Gore* bound for St. Christopher's.

John Ives, baptised 19 May 1727, son of John I., butcher; 16 January 1743 to his mother Sarah I. and Thomas Jones, broker, to serve Edward Jones of Antigua, merchant.

George Fish, baptised 31 August 1720, son of George F., grocer, admitted from St. Botolph Aldgate; 12 November 1737 to Robert Bostock, commander of the *Katherine* bound for Jamaica.

Thomas Durant, baptised 10 December 1721, son of William D., barber surgeon, admitted from Christ Church; 19 March 1737 to his said father and Mr. Slingsby Bethell to serve his brother-in-law Sir William Coddrington, merchant.

James Purchase, baptised 13 December 1722, son of Peter P., admitted from All Hallows Barking in the place of Robert Smith; 21 November 1737 to his brother-in-law John Knight of Giltspur Street and Clemens Chapman of All Hallows Barking, mariner, to serve Richard Rowland of St. Christopher's, merchant.

George Guy, baptised 11 July 1721, son of John G., admitted from Sherborne, Dorset, in the place of Daniel Hamblin; 14 January 1736 to Mr. Henry Sheppard on behalf of his mother Mary Hole and Mr. Thomas Strode of London, merchant, to serve Hon. Richard Sadler of Barbados, merchant.

Admissions in April 1731

Richard Jennings, baptised 29 March 1723, son of Thomas J., clockmaker, admitted from St. Andrew Holborn; 4 October 1737 to his uncle Richard Powell of Silver Street, Golden Square, and Richard Keech of Shoe Lane to serve Mordecai Booth of Gloucester County, Virginia, merchant.

William Langford, baptised 30 May 1726, son of William L., fishmonger, admitted from St. Mary Aldermary; 25 June 1742 to his said father to serve Thomas Summersett, Mr. of the *Carolina Packet* bound for Carolina.

Jonathan Poole, baptised 27 September 1722, son of John P., currier, admitted from St. Sepulchre; 17 August 1738 to his aunt Margaret Adams and godfather Oliver Humphreys to serve Thomas Laws, Mr. of the *Friendship* bound for Jamaica.

Peregrine Phillips, baptised 18 July 1725, son of Richard P., cooper, admitted from St. Botolph Bishopsgate; 13 March 1740 to his said father to serve Thomas Storer Esq. of Jamaica, merchant.

Charles Siddall, baptised 23 March 1722, son of George S., innholder, admitted from St. Bride's; 8 April 1736 to his mother Martha Murray to serve John Masters, merchant, in New England.

Lumley Woodyer, baptised 8 November 1724, son of Edward W., vintner, admitted from St. Bride's; 12 March 1740 to his friend Thomas Parry and Davy Breholt of London, merchant, to serve Sir William Pym of St. Christopher's, merchant.

Francis Marston, baptised 10 February 1721, son of Richard M., joiner, admitted from St. Margaret Westminster; 28 November 1735 to Mr. John Keith of London, merchant, to serve George Baseley of Spanish Town, Jamaica, merchant.

James Marsden, born 23 May 1721, son of Miles M., admitted from St. Dunstan in the West by order of Court; 20 October 1736 to his mother Mary Turner to serve Hugh Crawford, Mr. of the *Mermaid* bound for Jamaica.

James Butler Harris, baptised 7 January 1722, son of Butler H., admitted from St. Mary Aldermary; 3 December 1736 to his said father to serve Crispin Green of Bridge Town, Barbados, merchant.

John Prince, baptised 23 September 1722, son of William P., joiner, admitted from St. Giles in the Fields; 21 October 1737 to his uncle James P. and Beeston Long, merchant, to serve George Bullman of Savanna, Jamaica, merchant.

Joseph Bunn, baptised 4 April 1723, son of Henry B., admitted from Great Stanmore, Middlesex, by order of Court; 8 September 1739 with the consent of his said father to Mr. Henry Glover on behalf of Thomas Beckford of London, merchant, to serve Mrs. Jannet Hynes of Westmoreland,

Jamaica, widow, to learn the art of book-keeping and merchandizing.

Peter Gandy, baptised 16 October 1724, son of Peter G., admitted from St. Stephen Coleman Street in the place of John Cole deceased; 19 March 1740 to his said father and William Blackborn, Mr. of the *Gale*, to serve William Pusey of Jamaica, merchant.

Admissions in April 1732

Thomas Gardner, baptised 15 July 1722, son of Thomas G., joiner, admitted from St. Katherine Creechurch; 21 October 1737 to his cousin Grace Jones and Beeston Long, merchant, to serve William Cunningham of Savanna, Jamaica, merchant.

John Morley, baptised 25 April 1722, son of Thomas M., carpenter, admitted from St. James Clerkenwell; 29 January 1736 to his friend Peter Marriage of Cow Cross, victualler, to serve John Homans of Boston, New England, merchant.

Thomas Ward, baptised 12 February 1724, son of Thomas W., weaver, admitted from St. Mary Islington; 18 April 1740 to his mother Martha Heath and John Asgill, tobacconist of Newgate Street, to serve Richard Goslin of Barbados, merchant.

John Thorowgood Cole, baptised 21 January 1722, son of Benjamin C., haberdasher, admitted from St. Sepulchre; 21 October 1737 to his sister Elizabeth C. and Mr. David Currie, merchant, to serve Florentius Vassall of Jamaica, merchant.

John Denston, baptised 27 August 1721, son of William D., haberdasher, admitted from St. Andrew Holborn; 28 November 1735 to his aunt Elizabeth Wilcox and John Wilcox of Cannon Street, merchant, to serve Elizabeth Jordan of St. Elizabeth, Jamaica, merchant.

Charles Bromhall, baptised 27 June 1721, son of Matthias B., vintner, admitted from St. Andrew Holborn in the place of John Mattison; 14 January 1737 to Thomas Gordon, merchant of Tower Hill, and Slingsby Bethell, merchant, to serve John Vernon of St. Peter's, Antigua, planter.

Admissions in April 1733

William Sambach, baptised 25 August 1723, son of William S., plumber, admitted from St. Paul Covent Garden; 2 March 1739 to his cousin John Lloyd of Long Acre and Thomas Tryon of London, merchant, to serve William Furnell of Antigua, merchant.

John Haynes, baptised 15 May 1726, son of John H., butcher, admitted from St. Mary Whitechapel; 20 November 1740 to his mother Elizabeth Smith to serve Slingsby Bethell of London, merchant, in Antigua.

Jonathan Scott, baptised 28 January 1725, son of Walter S., cooper, admitted from St. Dunstan in the East; 8 November 1740 to John Dod Bonell, Mr. of the *Foxhunter* bound for Jamaica.

William James, baptised 15 October 1724, son of William J., cutler, admitted from St. Mary le Strand; 3 September 1740 to his friend Robert Caldwall of Marigold Court, Strand, and Papillon Ball of London, merchant, to serve William Gibbon of St. Christopher's, apothecary and surgeon.

Joseph How, baptised 30 June 1723, son of Joseph H., draper, admitted from St. Giles Cripplegate; 27 April 1738 to his mother Mary H. and Henry Lascelles, merchant, to serve Edward Lascelles Esq. of Barbados.

Henry Reeve, baptised 10 June 1722, son of Joseph R., farrier, admitted from St. Mary Colechurch; 10 February 1738 to his mother Ann R. and Mr. Henry Lascelles, merchant, to serve Richard Morecraft of Bridge Town, Barbados, merchant.

William Pyrton, baptised 8 November 1724, son of Richard P., admitted from St. Botolph Bishopsgate; 24 March 1740 to his mother Isabella P. and Henry Lang of Broad Street to serve Sir Simon Clark of Spanish Town, Jamaica.

Lionell Chasty, born 30 December 1723, son of Melchisideck C., admitted from St. James Westminster by order of Court; 2 June 1739 to his mother Clearanna C. to serve Francis Wightwick Esq. of the Middle Temple in Jamaica.

Charles Fletcher, baptised 19 April 1724, son of John F., stationer, admitted from Christ Church; 16 January 1739 to Edward and Thomas Fletcher and Roger Drake of London, merchant, to serve John Gale Esq. of Wittrywood, Jamaica, planter.

William Ball, baptised 27 August 1727, son of John B., poulterer, admitted from St. James Westminster; 30 March 1743 to his friend Mary Groves to serve Jonathan Greene, wholesale dealer in Jamaica.

Joseph Sheppard, baptised 9 November 1724, son of Isaac S., carpenter, admitted from St. Giles Cripplegate; 8 November 1740 to Daniel Mocher, Mr. of the *Neptune* bound for South Carolina.

Edward Marriott, baptised 11 June 1722, son of Benjamin M., grocer, admitted from Christ Church; 16 March 1738 to his said father and John Serocold, merchant, to serve Charles Price of Spanish Town, Jamaica, merchant.

Humphrey Wallis, baptised 27 August 1722, son of John W., fishmonger, admitted from St. Michael Queenhithe in the place of Charles Goodwin; 5 December 1737 to his said father to serve Humphrey Bell of Old Swan Lane, merchant, in Virginia.

William Lownds, born 30 June 1723, son of William L., admitted from St. Margaret Westminster in the place of Giles Hook, presented by the parish of St. James Clerkenwell; 16 October 1738 to his brother-in-law Jonathan Hawys to serve Darby Lux of Rotherhithe, Surrey, Mr. of the galley *Genoa* bound for Virginia.

William Haynes, born in December 1724, son of William H., carman, admitted from the Liberty of Norton Folgate; 14 February 1740 to his mother Dorothy H. to serve Mr. William Randolph of James River, Virginia.

James Williams, baptised 5 April 1727, son of James W., baker, admitted from St. Mildred Bread Street; 2 December 1741 to his mother Mary W. and George Dunbar of Gold Square, Crutched Friars, merchant, to serve Charles Dunbar of Antigua, merchant.

John Galwith Crumpler, baptised 21 October 1724, son of Samuel C., weaver, admitted from St. Dunstan Stepney; 19 May 1740 to William Playters, Mr. of the *Alexander* bound for New England.

Edmund Hampson, baptised 27 May 1724, son of Edward H., stationer, admitted from St. Giles Cripplegate; 18 March 1740 to his uncle James Worger and Mr. Samuel Travers of London, merchant, to serve Mr. Robert Henvill of St. Christopher's, merchant.

Richard Tyer, baptised 25 December 1726, son of Henry T., innholder, admitted from St. Stephen Coleman Street; 23 March 1742 to his mother Elizabeth Noyes and Mr. Thomas Lane of London, merchant, to serve Mr. Peter Faneuil of Boston, New England, merchant.

James Knewstubb, baptised 10 July 1726, son of Daniel K., embroiderer, admitted from St. Botolph Bishopsgate; 22 January 1742 to his mother Diana Glover and Thomas Kerby of London, merchant, to serve Stephen Blizard of Antigua, merchant.

Thomas Mills, baptised 22 January 1727, son of Richard M., salter, admitted from St. James Westminster; 16 February 1742 to his sister Ann M. and Mr. Beeston Long, merchant, to serve Mrs. Elizabeth Williams of Westmoreland, Jamaica, planter.

William Barber, baptised 14 March 1725, son of Joseph B., needlemaker, admitted from St. Michael Crooked Lane; 8 May 1740 to his brother Joseph B. to serve Humphrey Ball [signs *Bell*] of London, merchant, in Virginia.

Henry Batty, baptised 10 March 1723, son of Henry B., gunmaker, admitted from St. Katherine by the Tower; 26 May 1739 to Daniel Herbert, Mr. of the *Friendship* bound for Jamaica.

Thomas Stevens, baptised 29 September 1724, son of Thomas S., carman, admitted from St. Katherine Creechurch; 31 October 1740 to his said father and — Gearish of Mark Lane, merchant, to serve Edward Chester of Antigua, merchant.

Jonah Mills, baptised 17 December 1724, son of John M., merchant tailor, admitted from St. Martin in the Fields; 28 September 1739 to his mother Ann M. and Mr. Edward Athawes of London, merchant, to serve John Fairchild of Bridge Town, Barbados, merchant.

James Radaway, born 5 July 1726, son of James R., mercer, admitted from St. Dunstan in the West; 2 December 1742 to his friend James Carrington of Fetter Lane to serve William Reynolds, Mr. of the *Pretty Betsy* bound for Jamaica.

James Aiskell, baptised 5 March 1728, son of Poplay A., admitted from St. Andrew Holborn; 10 February 1744 to his father-in-law Vincent Edwards to serve Thomas Penn Esq., Proprietor of Pennsylvania.

Admissions in April 1735

William Antrobus, baptised 15 March 1728, son of John A., stationer, admitted from St. Vedast; 3 September 1741 to his friend Nathaniel Smith on behalf of his mother Mary Gurney and to Mr. Thomas Martin of London, merchant, to serve John Martin of Antigua, merchant.

Thomas Fish, baptised 12 November 1727, son of Robert F., barber surgeon, admitted from All Hallows Staining; [no date] to his mother Hannah F. to serve Mr. William Jenkins of Bridge Town, Barbados, merchant.

James Jones, baptised 10 November 1729, son of William J., admitted from Christ Church by order of Court; 8 June 1743 to Thomas Moncur, Mr. of the *Britannia* bound for St. Christopher's.

George Soames, baptised 2 January 1726, son of Henry S., tallow chandler, admitted from St. Dunstan in the West; 9 February 1741 to his mother Mary S. and Thomas Fell living near Shadwell Church to serve Samuel Smith of Barbados, merchant.

William Morris, baptised 8 August 1726, son of William M., butcher, admitted from St. Andrew Holborn; 24 October 1741 to William Story, Mr. of the galley *Sarah* bound for Carolina.

Robert Croker, baptised 12 September 1727, son of Thomas C., plasterer, admitted from St. Giles Cripplegate; 1 February 1742 to Mr. Robert Cary of London, merchant, to serve Lewis Burwell of James River, Virginia, merchant.

John Newman, baptised 6 January 1730, son of Edward N., joiner, admitted from St. Andrew Holborn; 19 December 1744 to his friend Mr. Edward Walmsley and Mr. George Barclay of London, merchant, to serve William Aikenhead Esq. of Jamaica.

Joseph Sterne, baptised 21 November 1728, son of Joseph S., barber surgeon, admitted from St. Dunstan in the West; 15 March 1744 to Thomas Beckford of London, merchant, to serve Peter Furnell of Jamaica, merchant.

Thomas Mason, baptised 12 July 1724, son of Thomas M., leatherseller, admitted from St. Martin in the Fields; 29 March 1740 with the consent of his friend William Smith of Long Acre, tallow chandler, to Mr. William Park of Foster Lane, tallow chandler, to serve Benjamin Dolbeare of Boston, New England, merchant.

John Salter, baptised 5 July 1727, son of Peter S., joiner, admitted from St. Botolph Aldgate; 23 December 1741 with the consent of his mother Jane S. to his uncle William Brook and Mr. Thomas Stroud of Great Ormond Street, merchant, to serve Hon. Richard Salter of Barbados, merchant.

George Brome, baptised 10 June 1727, son of George B., wax chandler, admitted from St. Andrew Holborn; 11 February 1742 with the consent of his aunt Mrs. Sarah Sulley to his cousin Mrs. Katherine Wright living at the *Rising Sun*, Cornhill, and Thomas Truman of London, merchant, to serve Stephen Adye of St. Christopher's, merchant.

Allen Townsend, baptised 28 January 1728, son of Edward T., dyer, admitted from Christ Church; 26 February 1743 to his mother Sarah Ramsey and Papillon Ball, merchant, to serve Benjamin Clifton of St. Christopher's, merchant.

Thomas Lambert, baptised 28 November 1725, son of John L., merchant tailor, admitted from St. Andrew Holborn; 24 October 1741 to Stephen Blanket, Mr. of the *Landovery* bound for Jamaica.

Samuel Elliott, baptised in September 1727, son of Thomas E., wax chandler, admitted from St. Mary Abchurch; 21 January 1743 to his mother Ann E. and Thomas Tryon, merchant, to serve William Furnell of Antigua, merchant.

Edmund Physick, baptised 28 May 1727, son of Timothy P., merchant tailor, admitted from St. Botolph Aldersgate; 19 February 1741 to his uncle Henry White of Great Eastcheap to serve Thomas Penn of Pennsylvania, merchant.

William Dallow, baptised 17 October 1727, son of William D., admitted from St. Botolph Bishopsgate by order of Court; 12 March 1742 to his aunt Mary Hanmore of Little Essex Street and Mr. David Currie, merchant, to serve Florentius Vassell Esq. of Jamaica.

Nathaniel Bird, baptised 18 November 1725, son of Nathaniel B., admitted from St. Giles Cripplegate by order of Court; 10 March 1740 to his sister Charlotte B. to serve Jeremiah Jones of Limehouse in New England.

William Smith, baptised 22 March 1726, son of William S., admitted from Whitefriars Precinct in the place of George Jones; 31 January 1731 to his uncle James S. to serve Micajah Perry Esq., merchant, in Virginia.

Michael Segers, baptised 29 October 1727, son of Michael S., admitted from St. James Westminster in the place of Andrew Searle; 26 April 1744 to his mother Mary S. to serve John Clark, Mr. of the *Argyle* bound for Virginia.

Admissions in April 1736

William Martindale, baptised 18 April 1732, son of William M., admitted from St. Gregory by order of Court; 9 December 1746 to his mother Harriot M. and Beeston Long, merchant, to serve Charles Long of Jamaica, merchant.

Samuel Say, born 29 June 1727, son of William S., cooper, admitted from Stepney; 10 May 1742 to his uncle Luke Porter, merchant in Mark Lane, to serve Robert Osborn of Barbados, merchant.

John Atwood, baptised 17 April 1727, son of John A., weaver, admitted from Christ Church; 23 November 1743 to his uncle Simon Julius to serve William Clarke, Mr. of the *New Industry* bound for Jamaica.

William Free, baptised 14 January 1728, son of Thomas F., draper, admitted from St. Olave Southwark; 18 February 1743 to Mr. Thomas Lane of Nicholas Lane, Lombard Street, merchant, to serve Mr. David Le Gallis of Boston, New England, merchant.

John Walford, baptised 18 January 1728, son of Tompson W., haberdasher, admitted from St. Saviour Southwark; 21 October 1742 to his grandfather John Brush to serve Thomas Johnson, Mr. of the *Parnassus* bound for Jamaica.

William Haines, baptised 10 February 1726, son of William H., wax chandler, admitted from St. Andrew Holborn; 7 November 1740 to his said father and Zachary Bourryan, merchant, to serve Edward Bourryan of St. Christopher's.

Richard Haskins, baptised 18 July 1727, son of Richard H., joiner, admitted from Holy Trinity Minories; 4 February 1742 to his said father and Beeston Long, merchant, to serve Thomas Fearon Esq. of Clarendon, Jamaica, planter.

William Townsend, baptised 21 June 1728, son of William T., barber surgeon, admitted from All Hallows Barking; 7 November 1743 to his uncle William Gladman of the *Golden Cock*, Snow Hill, to serve William Redhead of Antigua, merchant.

Richard Street, born 20 April 1726, son of Richard S., fishmonger, admitted from St. Sepulchre; 20 March 1742 to his mother Elizabeth S. and Edward Tyzack of London, merchant, to serve James Rodon of Kingston, Jamaica, merchant.

Richard Kello, baptised 24 June 1726, son of Samuel K., draper, admitted from St. Botolph Aldgate by order of Court; 3 February 1741 to his mother Mary K. and James Wray of Virginia, undertaker, to serve Edward Barradell of Williamsburgh, Attorney-General of Virginia.

Thomas Davis, baptised 10 October 1726, son of Thomas D., weaver, admitted from St. Paul Covent Garden; 8 September 1741 to Thomas Martin of Baldwin Court to serve Patrick Cussack of Antigua, planter.

Widmore Perry, born in November 1727, son of Henry P., admitted from Deptford, Kent, by order of Court; 26 March 1742 to his mother Susan P. and Mr. William Whitaker of London, merchant, to serve — Clark of Barbados, merchant.

Richard Lloyd, born in October 1728, son of Thomas L., haberdasher, admitted from St. Saviour Southwark;

18 February 1743 to his uncle Hugh L. and John Samuel, warehouseman of Basing Court, Lombard Street, to serve Philip Vanhorne of New York, merchant.

Samuel Kello, baptised 25 July 1725, son of Samuel K., draper, admitted from St. Katherine Creechurch; 15 April 1740 to his mother Mary K. and Mr. Robert Sedgwick of London, merchant, to serve Mr. Isaac Winslow of Boston, New England, merchant.

William Burrows, baptised 13 January 1726, son of William B., admitted from All Hallows Staining by order of Court; 4 August 1743 to his mother Mary Shiers and John Carruthers of London, merchant, to serve Chief Justice Whittaker of Carolina.

Richard Littleboy, baptised 27 May 1728, son of George L., cutler, admitted from St. Olave Silver Street by order of Court; 24 September 1743 to his said father to serve Michael Dod Jr. of Jamaica, merchant.

Richard Allnutt, baptised 19 May 1728, son of Edward A., joiner, admitted from St. Botolph Aldgate; 13 September 1743 to his uncle Richard A. and Mr. Thomas Parsons of London, merchant, to serve Francis Jones of Bermuda, merchant.

John Jerom, baptised 2 January 1729, son of John J., shipwright, admitted from Lambeth, Surrey; 13 October 1743 to his grandfather John Caton and James George Douglas of Broad Street, merchant, to serve John Douglas Esq. of St. Christopher's.

Francis Bird, baptised 25 February 1728, son of Francis B., weaver, admitted from Lambeth, Surrey; 7 May 1743 to William Playters, Mr. of the *Florentius* bound for Jamaica.

Admissions in April 1737

Joseph Garner, baptised 27 January 1728, son of Joseph G., innholder, admitted from St. Botolph Aldersgate; 12 November

1743 to Thomas Glover, Mr. of the *Bladen* bound for Virginia.

Richard Robinson, baptised 27 August 1727, son of Richard R., glover, admitted from St. Andrew Undershaft; 24 October 1741 to John Angwin, Mr. of the *Le Guinea* bound for Jamaica.

Francis James, baptised 1 March 1730, son of William J., admitted from Clapham, Surrey, by order of Court; 5 September 1744 to his mother Mary J. and Mr. George Maxwell of London, merchant, to serve Alexander Walker of Barbados, merchant.

John Bliss, baptised 26 October 1729, son of Benjamin B., fishmonger, admitted from St. Luke, Middlesex; 17 August 1744 to his aunt Frances B. and Mr. George Chandler of London, merchant, to serve Hampson Needham Esq. of Spanish Town, Jamaica.

James Webb, baptised 30 January 1726, son of Jacob W., joiner, admitted from St. Ann Westminster; 14 February 1741 to his uncle Henry Motlow to serve Elisha Johnson of Rhode Island, New England, Mr. of the *Bonetta*.

John Gore, baptised 27 November 1730, son of John G., admitted from St. Botolph Aldgate by order of Court; 27 March 1745 to his father-in-law Charles Stanton and Mr. Thomas Kerby of London, merchant, to serve Jonas Langford Esq. of Antigua.

Henry Powell, baptised 30 January 1729, son of Henry P., joiner, admitted from St. Andrew Holborn; 21 February 1744 to his uncle Richard P. and Mr. John Moorey of London, merchant, to serve William Mayo of Virginia, merchant.

Richard Reeves, baptised 22 November 1730, son of William R., tiler and bricklayer, admitted from Twickenham, Middlesex; 2 December 1745 to his friend Mr. Edward Holder of Ludgate Street, haberdasher, to serve James Dawkins of Jamaica, merchant.

William Polehampton, baptised 25 January 1727, son of Adam P., plasterer, admitted from St. John Southwark; 22 March 1743 to his sister Sarah Walmsley to serve Samuel Wragg of London, merchant, in Carolina.

William Complin, baptised 6 January 1730, son of Cornish C., vintner, admitted from All Saints & St. John, Hertford, by order of Court; 7 September 1744 to Thomas Sandford of London, merchant, to serve Silvester Gardiner of Boston, New England, surgeon and apothecary.

James Lowman, baptised 29 June 1730, son of Samuel L., carpenter, admitted from St. Andrew Holborn; 7 September 1744 to his mother Elizabeth L. and Mr. George Maxwell, merchant of Mincing Lane, to serve Mr. Alexander Walker of Barbados, merchant.

Robert Holloway, born 9 July 1731, son of Thomas H., waterman, admitted from St. Mary Rotherhithe, Surrey; 31 October 1746 to his sister Grace H. and Mr. William Whitaker of Tower Street, merchant, to serve Samuel Sedgwick of Barbados, apothecary and surgeon.

John Nickells, baptised 14 August 1727, son of John N., barber surgeon, admitted from Kensington, Middlesex; 12 March 1742 to his mother Mary N. and Mr. David Currie, merchant, to serve Florentius Vassell Esq. of Jamaica.

Thomas Smith, baptised 2 March 1729, son of Thomas S., admitted from St. Paul Shadwell by order of Court; 22 October 1742 to his uncle William S. and George Dunbar of London, merchant, to serve Walter Sydeserfe of Newington, Middlesex, merchant, in Antigua.

William Munk Summerly, baptised 17 November 1728, son of John S., skinner, admitted from Stepney in the place of Carlile Bradford; 19 March 1743 to George Wane, commander of the *Lovely Betty* bound for Jamaica.

Richard Wilmoth, baptised 1 January 1729, son of William W., admitted from Sherborne, Dorset, in the place of George Guy; 2 December 1742 to his friend Jonathan Forrest on behalf of his mother Mary W. to serve William Mayers of

St. Philip's, Barbados, merchant.

Gilbert Child, baptised 19 October 1729, son of Ralph C., cook, admitted from St. James Clerkenwell in the place of John Langhorn; 29 August 1744 to his grandmother Ann Edwards and Beeston Long, merchant, to serve John Thompson of Jamaica, merchant.

Admissions in April 1738

Edmund Gill, baptised 6 April 1728, son of Henry G., dyer; 23 October 1742 to his mother Sarah G. to serve John Houghton of South Carolina, merchant.

George Rivington, baptised 7 August 1730, son of William R., barber surgeon, admitted from St. Faith's; 24 May 1746 to William French, Mr. of the *Whitehall* bound for Jamaica.

Edward Lambert, baptised 29 August 1731, son of John L., merchant tailor, admitted from St. Andrew Hubbard; 11 August 1746 to his brother John L. of Finch Lane and Mr. Benjamin Ball to serve William Gibbons of St. Christopher's.

Matthew Hatch, baptised 13 April 1729, son of Matthew H., barber surgeon, admitted from St. Mary Magdalen Old Fish Street; 10 July 1744 to his said father and Mr. Beeston Long, merchant, to serve John Woollery of Jamaica, merchant.

John Hawthorne, baptised 13 March 1730, son of Henry H., clothworker, admitted from St. Luke, Middlesex; 30 July 1744 to his mother Mary H. and William Dunbar, merchant, to serve Walter Tullideph of Antigua, merchant.

William Tea, baptised 13 June 1729, son of John T., innholder, admitted from St. Andrew Holborn; 6 April 1745 to his mother Hannah Cole and Thomas Penn Esq. to serve William Peters of Pennsylvania, attorney at law.

Francis Hoare, baptised 27 July 1729, son of John H., joiner, admitted from St. Martin Orgar; 19 November 1743 to Thomas Johnson, Mr. of the *Parnassus* bound for Jamaica.

William Poole, baptised 14 May 1731, son of Barnham P., vintner, admitted from St. Mary Whitechapel; 6 November 1746 to his said father and Thomas Tryon Esq., merchant, to serve Ashton Warner Esq. of Antigua.

John Osborn, baptised 17 November 1728, son of Samuel O., shipwright, admitted from West Ham, Essex; 23 May 1744 to Thomas Collett, Mr. of the *Albinia* bound for Jamaica.

Henry Proctor, baptised 3 June 1730, son of Francis P., admitted from Long Preston, Yorkshire; 27 March 1740 to Mr. Thomas Warren of Bartholomew Lane to serve — Mitchell of Jamaica, merchant.

Thomas Haley, baptised 3 January 1731, son of James H., weaver, admitted from St. Dunstan in the West; 4 February 1746 to his mother Elizabeth Garry to serve Mr. Richard Bateman of Jamaica, merchant.

Edward Birchett, baptised 18 February 1729, son of Edward B., gunmaker, admitted from St. Margaret Westminster; 25 May 1744 to his mother Abigal B. and Mr. Jonathan Ewer of Hatton Garden, merchant, to serve Hon. John Stewart of Jamaica, merchant.

William Gaylor, baptised 11 February 1731, son of John G., admitted from Denham, Buckinghamshire, by order of Court; 12 December 1746 to his cousin Thomas Alden to serve John Sutcliffe, Mr. of the *Feaxon* bound for Jamaica.

Sampson Facey, baptised 27 December 1729, son of Thomas F., admitted from Deptford, Kent, in the place of John Warren, presented by St. Dunstan in the East; 4 December 1744 to the mother Elizabeth F. and Thomas Shickle of Gracechurch Street, stationer, to serve John Shickle of Jamaica, merchant.

Admissions in April 1739

John Musgrove, baptised 27 September 1730, son of William M., admitted from Croydon, Surrey, by order of Court; 10 February 1746 to his said father to serve Oliver Dellance of New York, merchant.

George Dunbrack, baptised 5 September 1731, son of Thomas D., haberdasher, admitted from St. John the Baptist; 6 March 1747 to Samuel Pennant of London, merchant, to serve John Pennant Esq. of Savile Row in Jamaica.

John Stokes, baptised 29 March 1731, son of John S., farrier, admitted from St. Sepulchre; 16 January 1747 to his mother Catherine S. and James Knight of Stoke Newington, Middlesex, merchant, to serve John Lewis Esq. of Westmoreland, Jamaica.

William Eales, baptised 19 December 1731, son of William E., baker, admitted from St. Giles Cripplegate; 1 October 1746 to his mother Elizabeth E. and William Dunbar, merchant, to serve Walter Tullideph Esq. of Antigua.

Henry Johnson, baptised 16 February 1730, son of Henry J., carman, admitted from St. Botolph Aldgate; 19 February 1745 to his mother Sarah J. and Thomas Tryon, merchant, to serve James Weatherill of St. Christopher's and to learn book-keeping.

Charles Paine, baptised 28 December 1732, son of Thomas P., joiner, admitted from St. Botolph Bishopsgate; 14 November 1747 to George Wigg, Mr. of the *New Industry* bound for Jamaica.

John Head, baptised 27 April 1732, son of Joseph H., joiner, admitted from St. Gregory by St. Paul's; 19 November 1747 to his mother Hester Woodall and Oliver Noyes of London, merchant, to serve John Gohram of Boston, New England.

Richard Sheppard, born in June 1729, son of Richard S., draper, admitted from St. Luke, Middlesex; 24 November 1744 to Owen Fergus, Mr. of the *Volunteer* bound for Montserrat.

Thomas Chamberlayne Amory, baptised 12 January 1732, son of William A., draper, admitted from Greenwich, Kent; 3 June 1747 to his mother Rose A. to serve Mr. William Booth of Virginia, merchant.

William Goldar, baptised 10 November 1729, son of Josiah G., grocer, admitted from Whitefriars Precinct; 23 May 1744 to Edward Oliver, Mr. of the galley *Ann* bound for Jamaica.

James Perry, baptised 18 June 1731, son of James P., clothworker, admitted from St. Martin in the Fields; 22 November 1746 to Thomas B—-nett, Mr. of the *Pompey* bound for Jamaica.

William Blake, born in May 1731, son of Richard B., admitted from St. Olave Southwark by order of Court; 24 April 1746 to his said father to serve Samuel Cary, merchant of the *Gainsborough* bound for St. Christopher's.

Lemuel Lowe, born 4 October 1729, son of Thomas L., admitted from St. Sepulchre; 1 June 1745 to Charles Smyter, Mr. of the galley *Philadelphia* bound for Philadelphia.

Richard Hudson, born 12 February 1732, son of John H., admitted from St. Olave Southwark; 1 February 1748 to his sister Mary Lloyd to serve Joseph Winwood of Somerset Street, woolstapler; revoked as the sister Lloyd was unwell and at the request of his half-sister Elizabeth Ludlam bound to Mr. Richard Boddicott of London, merchant, to serve Joseph Lyons Esq. of Antigua.

Admissions in April 1740

Charles Whitehead, baptised 26 April 1729, son of Charles W., glover, admitted from St. Andrew Holborn; 16 November 1743 to James Brown, Mr. of the *Biddy* bound for Antigua.

George Henry Dwight, baptised in February 1734, son of John D., scrivener, admitted from St. Michael Bassishaw; 10 March 1749 to his uncle Mr. Thomas Northey to serve

Nathaniel Bascome, Mr. of the *Rebecca* bound for Bermuda.

Richard Gardin, baptised 28 January 1733, son of Tudor G., haberdasher, admitted from St. Leonard Foster Lane; 16 March 1749 to his cousin William Winter to serve Martin Read of Ramsgate, Kent, Mr. of the *Haughton* bound for Jamaica.

Samuel Spragg, baptised 17 November 1731, son of William S., leatherseller, admitted from St. Mary Mounthaw; 27 October 1747 to his said father and Beeston Long, merchant, to serve Hon. Robert Penny, Attorney-General of Jamaica.

John Coates, born 20 March 1733, son of William C., cooper, admitted from St. James Clerkenwell; 27 October 1747 to his mother Elizabeth C. and Alexander Grant of London, merchant, to serve Major-General Charles Dawes of Jamaica, merchant.

William Leacock, baptised 8 November 1730, son of John L., weaver, admitted from St. Mary Newington, Surrey; 26 February 1747 to his father-in-law Gabriel Knight and Samuel Turner of London, merchant, to serve Jacob Thibou of Antigua, merchant.

William Glen, born 28 July 1728, son of Mary G., freewoman of London, merchant tailor, admitted from St. Mary Rotherhithe, Surrey, by order of Court; 7 October 1743 to his said mother and Thomas Kerby of Billiter Square, merchant, to serve Thomas Warner of Antigua.

John Norris, baptised 24 January 1734, son of Robert N., merchant tailor, admitted from St. Mary le Bow; 31 May 1750 to William Wallcott, Mr. of the *Lovely Lass* bound for Barbados.

John Noys, baptised 21 March 1733, son of Charles N., admitted from St. Botolph Aldersgate by order of Court; 16 November 1747 to his friend Mr. Edward Busby to serve Robert Bowman of Whitehaven, [Cumberland], Mr. of the

Britannia bound for Virginia.

James Smith, baptised 1 March 1732, son of John S., painter stainer, admitted from St. Michael Cornhill; 9 October 1747 to his mother Frances S. and George Chandler of London, merchant, to serve Mr. Samuel Whitehall of Spanish Town, Jamaica.

Constable Hassell Arnold, baptised 28 January 1734, son of John A., stationer, admitted from St. Dunstan in the West; 9 February 1748 to his said father and Mr. Richard Boddington of London, merchant, to serve William McKinnen Esq. of Antigua.

Richard Tea, baptised 23 September 1731, son of John T., innholder, admitted from St. Andrew Holborn by order of Court; 19 August 1746 to his mother Hannah Cole and Thomas Penn Esq. to serve William Parsons, Surveyor-General of Pennsylvania.

Richard Morrison, baptised 20 October 1732, son of David M., admitted from Cheshunt, Hertfordshire, by order of Court; 22 November 1746 to Francis Rasbury, Mr. of the *Scroop* bound for St. Christopher's.

John Farson, baptised 8 July 1731, son of James F., armourer and brazier, admitted from St. Martin in the Fields; 7 July 1746 to his mother Alice F. and Mr. Marmaduke Hilton of London, merchanrt, to serve Francis Wightwick Esq. of St. Dorothy's, Jamaica.

Nathan Treadway, born in January 1731, son of Nathan T., carpenter, admitted from All Hallows Barking; 6 December 1746 to his brother James T. and Thomas Tryon Esq., Treasurer of the Society for the Propagation of the Gospel, to serve the Society at Coddrington College in Barbados as book-keeper and schoolmaster.

Roger Clark, born in September 1732, son of John C., admitted from St. Dunstan in the West; 5 October 1747 to his said father to serve [blank] Lamton of Charles Town, South Carolina, merchant.

Edward Blood, baptised 23 July 1732, son of Robert B., admitted from Burton, Staffordshire; 7 December 1747 to his uncle Francis Wilson and Beeston Long, merchant, to serve Thomas Fearon Jr. of Clarendon, Jamaica.

Admissions in April 1741

Thomas Shene Kime, baptised 10 February 1733, son of William K., pattenmaker, admitted from St. Botolph Aldgate; 23 October 1747 to his mother Margaret K. and Thomas Parsons of the Crown Office, Middle Temple, to serve Francis Jones of Bermuda, merchant.

Turney Phillips, baptised 12 December 1731, son of John P., admitted from St. Michael Cornhill by order of Court; 3 November 1746 to his mother Anna P. and Robert Willock of Rainbow Coffee House, Cornhill, merchant, to serve William Lindsay Esq. of Spanish Town, Clerk of the Crown in Jamaica.

John Jackson, baptised 6 March 1732, son of William J., tallow chandler, admitted from St. Botolph Aldersgate; 3 February 1748 to his brother William J. and Willard Dunbar of London, merchant, to serve Walter Sydserfe Esq. of Antigua.

William Hall, baptised 17 February 1733, son of Silvester H., glover, admitted from St. Botolph Bishopsgate; 19 November 1748 to Robert Manly, Mr. of the *Elizabeth* bound for Barbados.

Robert Fowle, baptised 30 January 1733, son of Henry F., grocer, admitted from St. Saviour Southwark; 29 June 1748 to Solomon Goad, Mr. of the *St. John* bound for Jamaica.

Andrew Sutherland, born in October or November 1731, son of Robert S., admitted by order of Court; 1 October 1746 to his friend James McDermott of Adlam's Coffee House, Lincolns Inn Fields, and William Dunbar of London, merchant, to serve John Dunbar Esq. of Antigua.

James Walker, baptised 2 January 1733, son of Thomas W., admitted from St. Paul's, Bedford, by order of Court; 1 December 1747 to his cousin Thomas Spenceley to serve Robert Bowman, Mr. of the *Britannia* bound for Virginia.

Robert Hall, baptised 1 April 1734, son of Robert H., joiner, admitted from Richmond, Surrey; 3 November 1748 to his friend John Wicks of Queen Street, Cheapside, on behalf of his grandfather Baptist Hall, and to Beeston Long, merchant, to serve John Gale Esq. of Clarendon, Jamaica.

John Walnar, baptised 8 January 1734, son of William W., coachmaker, admitted from St. James Westminster; 14 November 1749 to Mr. John Bowden on behalf of his friend Mrs. Frith Clarkson, and Alexander Grant of London, merchant, to serve Major-General Charles Dawes of Jamaica, merchant.

Peter Verstille, baptised 10 August 1732, son of William V., carpenter, admitted from St. Luke, Middlesex; 20 March 1747 to his uncle Peter V. of Carpenters' Hall to serve Samuel Hughes of Boston, New England, merchant.

William Metcalf, baptised 16 October 1732, son of William M., admitted from St. Clement Danes by order of Court; 13 December 1746 to his friend Mr. Oliver Edwards of the Six Clerks' Office to serve Richard Higginson, Mr. of the *Mary* bound for Jamaica.

William Howard, baptised 29 November 1730, son of William H., baker, admitted from St. Clement Danes; 10 March 1746 to Mr. George Maxwell of London, merchant, to serve John Frere Esq. of Barbados.

George Parker, baptised 10 October 1731, son of John P., cooper, admitted from St. Katherine Coleman Street; 31 May 1746 to John Read, Mr. of the *Indian Queen* bound for Antigua.

Admissions in April 1742

John Pechey, baptised 10 April 1732, son of Daniel P., admitted from Harrow on the Hill, Middlesex, by order of Court; 25 February 1747 to Mr. Richard Charlton on behalf of the mother and to Anthony Hodges Esq. of Lincolns Inn Fields to serve Anthony Guichard of St. Christopher's, merchant.

George Unet, baptised 19 July 1737, son of Richard U., stationer, admitted from St. Mary's, Stafford; 26 September 1752 to his friend Mr. John Johnson on behalf of his aunt Sarah U. and to Thompson Hicks of Epsom, Surrey, gent, to serve Richard Lytcotts Esq. of Nevis.

John Day, baptised 12 August 1733, son of John D., wax chandler, admitted from St. James Garlickhithe; 3 February 1748 to his mother Lydia D. to serve Mr. John Holliday of Antigua, merchant.

Thomas Batty, baptised 20 December 1732, son of Henry B., gunmaker, admitted from St. John Wapping; 19 November 1748 to John Coulthurst, Mr. of the *St. George* bound for St. Christopher's.

John Moore, baptised 14 October 1733, son of John M., pattenmaker, admitted from All Hallows the Great; 3 March 1749 to his mother Ruth M. to serve Henry Livingston of Antigua, merchant.

James Barnard, baptised 27 March 1733, son of Thomas B., haberdasher, admitted from St. Leonard Shoreditch; 14 November 1747 to John Wade, Mr. of the *St. Ferdinando* bound for Jamaica.

Robert Corpe, baptised 3 November 1732, son of Robert C., admitted from Sherborne, Dorset, in the place of Robert Wilmoth; 12 September 1747 to his said father to serve Thomas Nelme, Mr. of the *Sally* bound for Bermuda.

Admissions in April 1743

Peter Searle, baptised 10 August 1739, son of John S., admitted from St. Martin Ludgate by order of Court; 27 July 1754 to Peter Hall, Mr. of the *Sandy Point* bound for the West Indies.

James Nabes, baptised 18 June 1732, son of William N., goldsmith, admitted from St. Leonard Foster Lane; 17 December 1747 to his mother Sarah N. and Beeston Long, merchant, to serve Thomas Fearon Jr. of Clarendon, Jamaica, planter.

William Strong, baptised 18 November 1732, son of David S., wire drawer, admitted from St. Luke, Middlesex; 15 January 1748 to his uncle John Perkins, notary public, and Thomas Kerby of London, merchant, to serve John Bannister of Antigua, merchant.

Jonathan Chandler, baptised 8 November 1730, son of Jonathan C., merchant tailor, admitted from St. Saviour Southwark; 18 February 1745 to his said father and Thomas Tryon, merchant, to serve Ashton Warner Esq. of Antigua.

Thomas Jackson, baptised 15 October 1732, son of Richard J., girdler, admitted from St. Giles Cripplegate; 22 November 1746 to Charles Smyter, Mr. of the *Burlington* bound for Philadelphia.

Cuthbert Potts, baptised 25 November 1737, son of Charles P., admitted from Chelsea, Middlesex; 23 September 1753 to his friend Mr. John Rice to serve Mr. James Gordon of Kingston, Jamaica, merchant.

Richard Townsend, baptised 31 March 1734, son of John T., clothworker, admitted from St. Sepulchre; 15 May 1751 to John Carlton, Mr. of the *Vernon* bound for Jamaica.

George Cobham, baptised 4 April 1736, son of John C., admitted from St. Martin in the Fields; 22 April 1752 to William Nicholson, Mr. of the galley *Beckford* bound for the West Indies.

John Walker, baptised 25 January 1734, son of Job W., mason, admitted from St. Mary Bothaw; 31 May 1750 to William

Reynolds, Mr. of the *Founthill* bound for Jamaica.

Richard Clark, baptised 26 August 1735, son of Richard C., blacksmith, admitted from St. Sepulchre; 4 February 1751 to his mother Barbara C. and Henry Hancock of London, merchant, to serve Walter Tullideph Esq. of Antigua.

William Lovejoy, baptised 28 September 1735, son of William L., admitted from Caversham, Oxfordshire, by order of Court; 18 March 1751 to his uncle James Peirson and Beeston Long, merchant, to serve Edward Morant Esq. of Jamaica.

John Dawes, born 30 April 1736, son of John D., admitted from St. James Clerkenwell by order of Court; 9 July 1751 to Mr. John Bowden on behalf of his friend Mrs. Sarah Yeo and to Mr. George Barclay of London, merchant, to serve Mr. William Aikenhead Esq. of Jamaica.

Robert Davenport, baptised 14 November 1735, son of John D., poulterer, admitted from St. Marylebone; 18 September 1750 to his grandmother Alice Herbert and John East of Gracechurch Street to serve John Harvey of Bermuda, merchant.

John Alchorn, baptised 8 November 1735, son of William A., glover, admitted from St. Christopher le Stocks; 22 February 1750 to his father-in-law Peter Grantham and Samuel Eaton, goldsmith of Wood Street, to serve Matthias Holst of Bridgetown, Barbados, jeweller.

George Clemason, baptised 5 February 1736, son of George C., joiner, admitted from St. Ann Blackfriars; 29 January 1751 to his cousin George C. of Ropemaker Alley, Moorfields, and aunt Ann Wright of Goswell Street and Beeston Long, merchant, to serve Richard Cargill Esq. of Jamaica.

Benjamin Allen, baptised 27 January 1734, son of Edward A., stationer, admitted from St. Mary Whitechapel; 11 November 1749 to his uncle Henry Slater of the Red Mead near the Hermitage and Beeston Long, merchant, to serve Henry Dawkins Esq. of Jamaica.

William Adams, baptised 17 June 1733, son of William A., glazier, admitted from St. Mary Whitechapel; 13 December 1748 to Elizabeth Grimston of Rosemary Lane and John East, merchant, to serve Thomas Gilbert Esq. of Bermuda, merchant.

John Hawkins, born 20 February 1736, son of Thomas H., admitted from St. Clement Danes by order of Court; 18 December 1751 to his friend Mr. Andrew Guertz of Nicholas Lane and Beeston Long, merchant, to serve George Ricketts Esq. of Jamaica, planter.

Thomas Fletcher, baptised 7 February 1733, son of Thomas F., founder, admitted from St. Botolph Aldgate; 17 February 1749 to his aunt Martha Brayley to serve Ambrose Judd, Mr. of the *Neptune* bound for Maryland.

William Lockwood, baptised 16 October 1732, son of Samuel L., admitted from St. Martin in the Fields by order of Court; 29 June 1748 to John Dod Bonell, Mr. of the *Beckford* bound for Jamaica.

David Glyster, baptised 13 January 1740, son of Thomas G., carpenter, admitted from St. Mary Whitechapel; 10 January 1756 to Henry Lusby, Mr. of the *Sally* bound for Antigua.

William Mould, baptised 14 May 1735, son of John M., admitted from St. James Clerkenwell in the place of Thomas Ancell; 15 February 1750 to his mother Hester M. and Samuel Storke of London, merchant, to serve William Dorrell of Salt River, Jamaica, merchant.

Admissions in April 1744

James Holyhead, baptised 16 April 1734, son of Thomas H., admitted from Speen, Buckinghamshire, by order of Court; 20 June 1747 to Thomas Parsons, Mr. of the *Hester* bound for Bermuda.

John Weadley, baptised 15 December 1734, son of John W., glover, admitted from St. Andrew Holborn; 5 February

1751 to his cousin Elizabeth Lathbury and Thomas Truman of London, merchant, to serve Sir Simon Clark of Jamaica.

James Barnard, baptised 13 October 1734, son of Joseph B., paviour, admitted from St. Stephen Coleman Street; 11 December 1749 to Mr. Jonathan Ewer of London, merchant, to serve Mark Hall Esq. of Jamaica, merchant.

James James, baptised 30 October 1734, son of Phillip J., admitted from St. Giles in the Fields by order of Court; 19 November 1748 to Henry Glendenny, Mr. of the *William* bound for Jamaica.

John Rose, baptised 8 January 1739, son of Thomas R., weaver, admitted from St. Ann Blackfriars; 22 March 1753 to his uncle Mr. John Landman and Mr. Thomas Warner of Antigua, counsellor at law, to serve Daniel Warner of Antigua, merchant.

John Wadham, baptised 2 April 1737, son of John W., clothworker, admitted from St. Mary Magdalen Bermondsey; 21 October 1752 to Richard Wiseham, Mr. of the *Banister* bound for St. Christopher's.

Josiah Warren, baptised 9 June 1736, son of Miles W., clothworker, admitted from Great Burstead, Essex; 29 January 1753 to his aunt Elizabeth W. of the China Shop, Pall Mall, to be bound to her brother Mr. Dominick W., chinaman of St. James's parish, to serve William Reed of Jamaica, merchant.

Nathaniel Exley, baptised 6 September 1736, son of Ester E., freewoman of London, merchant tailor, admitted from St. Clement Danes; 27 September 1751 to his grandfather Nathaniel Fermin of St. Clement Danes to serve Mr. Thomas Woolford Jr. of Barbados, merchant.

Christopher Cotterell, baptised 11 December 1735, son of Christopher C., admitted from St. Andrew Holborn by order of Court; 17 September 1751 to his father-in-law

Isaac Walton to serve Thomas Hunt, Mr. of the *Prince of Orange* bound for Bermuda.

Admissions in April 1745

Richard Augustus Yates, baptised 24 January 1735, son of Richard Y., admitted from Bromley, Kent, by order of Court; [?date] with the consent of his friend James Whitchurch Esq. to Edward Martin on behalf of George Arnold Esq. to serve Joseph Read of New York, merchant.

Robert Bignall, baptised 18 January 1739, son of Richard B., admitted from Hammersmith, Middlesex, by order of Court; 11 February 1754 to his mother Sarah B. and Robert Cary Esq., merchant, to serve David Mead Esq. of Virginia, merchant.

Thomas Longest, born 26 March 1736, son of Peter L., admitted from St. Peter's, Colchester, Essex, by order of Court; 2 December 1749 to Thomas Burck, Mr. of the *Montique* bound for Jamaica.

James Swift, baptised 21 April 1735, son of James S., admitted from St. Giles in the Fields by order of Court; 14 June 1751 to his mother Judith S. to serve Samuel Wade, Mr. of the *Sarah* bound for New England.

Richard Middleton, baptised 25 December 1733, son of Thomas M., leatherseller, admitted from St. Luke, Middlesex; 22 April 1749 to his mother Ann M. and George Chandler, merchant, to serve Benjamin Hume Esq. of Jamaica.

Charles Crouch, baptised 8 November 1736, son of John C., admitted from St. Mary Whitechapel by order of Court; 2 August 1751 to his guardian Mr. Nathaniel Hammond of the Bank and Mr. Richard Maitland of London, merchant, to serve Andrew Lessly of Antigua, merchant.

John Earl, baptised 12 September 1737, son of John E., admitted from St. Giles in the Fields by order of Court; 8 November 1752 to his friend Mr. Robert Cook and Mr. Beeston Long, merchant, to serve Hon. Samuel Long of

Jamaica, planter.

William Davis, baptised 22 February 1737, son of James D., clockmaker, admitted from St. James Clerkenwell; 21 October 1752 to Patrick White, Mr. of the *Sally* bound for Maryland.

James Ryan, baptised 19 February 1735, son of James R., currier, admitted from St. Saviour Southwark; 29 November 1749 to his said father and Mr. John Serocold, merchant, to serve Col. Charles Price of Jamaica.

Charles Munns, baptised 4 March 1737, son of William M., cook, admitted from St. Botolph Bishopsgate; 21 January 1751 to his mother Isabella M. to serve Richard Bennett, Mr. of the *Swift* bound for Antigua.

Admissions in April 1746

Thomas Sowell, baptised 13 July 1736, son of John S., baker, admitted from St. Bride's; 13 December 1751 to his mother Johanna S. and Mr. George Chandler, merchant, to serve Mr. Edmund Hide of Jamaica, merchant.

James Over, baptised 27 January 1735, son of Robert O., weaver, admitted from St. Leonard Shoreditch; 15 January 1750 to his mother Elizabeth O. and Thomas Mapstone of St. George in the East, Middlesex, mariner, to serve James Butler Harris of Barbados, merchant.

Robert Hagger, baptised 6 March 1737, son of Robert H., dyer, admitted from Christ Church; 21 October 1752 to Andrew Caside, Mr. of the *Caroline* bound for Carolina.

Joseph Sanders, baptised in January 1737, son of Joseph S., joiner, admitted from St. Ann Blackfriars; 29 July 1751 to his mother Elizabeth S. and Mr. John East, merchant, to serve Cornelius Hinson of Bermuda, merchant.

Samuel Smith, baptised 13 August 1741, son of Nathaniel S., waterman and lighterman, admitted from Dartford, Kent; 24 November 1755 to his mother Mary S. to serve Robert Rochfort of Jamaica, merchant.

William Emerson, baptised 4 November 1739, son of Christopher E., loriner, admitted from St. Bartholomew the Great; 25 January 1755 to serve Mr. Joseph Sproston of Kingston, Jamaica, merchant.

Joseph Tipson, baptised 10 October 1736, son of William T., haberdasher, admitted from St. Bartholomew the Great; 4 December 1751 to his uncle Mr. Joseph Crish and Mr. Samuel Eaton, goldsmith of Hoggin Lane, Wood Street, to serve Mr. Matthias Holst of Bridgetown, Barbados, jeweller and goldsmith.

William Taylor, baptised 6 April 1740, son of William T., woolman, admitted from St. Ann Blackfriars; 15 October 1754 to his uncle Daniel Masemore to serve Mr. James Pharaoh of Jamaica, merchant.

Phillip Fell, baptised 7 June 1738, son of Benjamin F., founder, admitted from St. Ann Blackfriars; 21 October 1752 to Robert Manly, Mr. of the *New Elizabeth* bound for Barbados.

James Purser, baptised 16 May 1737, son of James P., joiner, admitted from St. Bartholomew the Great; 9 June 1753 to Isham Randolph, Mr. of the *Anna* bound for Virginia.

John Lycett, baptised 2 October 1738, son of William L., horner, admitted from All Hallows London Wall; 6 March 1754 to his aunt Catherine Venables to serve Patrick Wilson of Antigua, goldsmith.

Admissions in April 1747

Alexander Toogood, baptised 15 April 1739, son of William T., admitted from Cheshunt, Hertfordshire, by order of Court; 23 January 1754 to his uncle Alexander Curtis and John East, merchant, to serve Thomas Gilbert of Bermuda, merchant.

John Smith, baptised 28 October 1739, son of John S., cordwainer, admitted from St. Botolph Bishopsgate; 14 July 1756 to William White, Mr. of the *Charming Nancy* bound for South Carolina.

John Mason, baptised 28 August 1738, son of John M., carman, admitted from All Hallows the Great; 7 August 1753 to his father-in-law Richard Hudson to serve Charles Payne, Mr. of the *Friendship* bound for Nevis.

James Woodason, baptised 12 January 1738, son of Thomas W., admitted from St. Benet Paul's Wharf by order of Court; 11 January 1752 to Mr. Joseph Bentley, wigmaker of Bagnio Lane, Newgate Street, to serve Col. Richard Lee of South Potomack, Virginia, Naval Officer.

John Droste, baptised 14 June 1739, son of John D., coachmaker, admitted from St. Martin in the Fields; 1 June 1754 to Richard Burton, Mr. of the *Myrtilla* bound for Philadelphia.

John Pimm, baptised 22 January 1738, son of Richard P., plumber, admitted from St. Olave Old Jewry; 14 April 1753 to his mother Elizabeth Wager and Beeston Long, merchant, to serve Hon. Samuel Long of Jamaica, planter.

Thomas Maddey, baptised 8 September 1737, son of George M., admitted from St. Martin in the Fields by order of Court; 8 November 1752 to his uncle Thomas Marlton and Beeston Long, merchant, to serve Thomas Foster Esq. of Jamaica, planter.

Anthony Blamire, baptised 26 May 1737, son of John B., admitted from Penrith, Cumberland, by order of Court; 26 October 1752 to his friend Mr. Thomas Blamire and Mr. William Bowden of London, merchant, to serve Mr. Anthony Walker Jr. of Virginia, merchant.

Thomas Bayley, baptised 21 September 1740, son of Thomas B., haberdasher, admitted from St. Giles Cripplegate; 7 July 1755 to his mother Sarah Church and Amos Avery of St. Giles Cripplegate, watchmaker, to serve Walrond Fearon Esq. of Jamaica, merchant.

Robert Smith, baptised 16 December 1737, son of John S., admitted from Woolverstone, Suffolk, by order of Court; 1 March 1754 to his aunt Mary S. and Robert Wigston of London, merchant, to serve Mrs. Mary Morant of Jamaica, planter.

Thomas Grigg, baptised 3 May 1741, son of Thomas G., admitted from St. Martin in the Fields by order of Court; 10 September 1757 to Charles Payne, Mr. of the *Prospect* bound for Nevis.

Jonathan Nabbs, baptised 30 November 1739, son of William N., goldsmith, admitted from St. Leonard Foster Lane; 17 January 1754 to his uncle Mr. John Burn and Mr. Nicholas Maitland of London, merchant, to serve John Gunthorpe of Antigua, merchant.

Thomas Bellasyse, baptised 12 December 1736, son of Richard B., sdmitted from St. Clement Danes by order of Court; 29 July 1751 to his said father and Mr. John East, merchant, to serve Joseph Vesey of Bermuda, merchant.

John Acourt, baptised 24 December 1737, son of John A., grocer, admitted from St. Andrew Hubbard; 10 January 1753 to his uncle Mr. Giles Theyer to serve Col. Francis Willis of Gloucester County, Virginia, merchant.

William Rawlings, baptised 27 September 1739, son of Christopher R., draper, admitted from St. Andrew Holborn; 2 March 1754 to his mother Hannah R. and Mr. Richard Maitland, merchant, to serve Anthony Wharton Esq. of St. Christopher's, merchant and planter.

Thomas Cannon, baptised 21 February 1739, son of George C., admitted from Walthamstow, Essex, by order of Court; 11 February 1754 to his brother George C. and William Hargraves on behalf of Mr. Nathaniel Bassnett of London, merchant, to serve Andrew Lessly of Antigua, merchant.

William Young, born in January 1736, son of Wicks Y., admitted from St. James Westminster by order of Court; 1 November 1751 to John Woodward, Mr. of the *Harrison* bound for Barbados.

James Thomas, baptised 19 March 1736, son of David T., admitted from St. Martin in the Fields by order of Court; 27 October 1750 to Thomas Latchford, commander of the *Mediterranean* bound for Jamaica.

Admissions in April 1748

James Thorowgood, baptised 3 September 1738, son of William T., glover, admitted from St. John the Baptist; 22 December 1753 to Adam Spencer Jr., Mr. of the *Galloway* bound for Maryland.

John Matthew Grove, baptised 2 October 1739, son of John G., dyer, admitted from St. Giles Cripplegate; 7 December 1753 to his mother Johanna G. and Mr. John Marratt to serve Mr. John Westcott, merchant, at St. Christopher's.

John Wright, born in December 17—, son of James W., admitted from St. Andrew Holborn by order of Court; 5 September 1755 to his mother Susannah W. and Robert Wigston of London, merchant, to serve John Pennant Esq. of Westmoreland, Jamaica.

Thomas Raffles, baptised 18 December 1737, son of Thomas R., admitted from St. Ann Blackfriars by order of Court; 27 January 1754 to his said father and Alexander Grant, merchant, to serve Capt. George Johnston of Jamaica, merchant.

Thomas Horne, baptised 28 August 1741, son of William H., poulterer, admitted from Birmingham, Warwickshire, by order of Court; 22 July 1756 to his friend Mr. Thomas Horne and Mr. Richard Maitland, merchant, to serve Mr. Anthony Wharton of St. Christopher's, merchant.

Zachariah White, baptised 8 January 1738, son of Zachariah W., goldsmith, admitted from St. Olave Silver Street; 11 August 1753 to his father-in-law Jonas Harris to serve William White, Mr. of the *Charming Nancy* bound for South Carolina.

John Drinkwater, baptised 29 June 1739, son of Edmond D., glover, admitted from Holy Trinity; 14 December 1754 to his mother Mary D. and John Porter Esq. to serve Mr. John Stephens of Spanish Town, Jamaica, merchant.

Richard Garland, baptised 28 April 1737, son of John G., draper, admitted from All Hallows on the Wall; 18 March 1752 to his mother Elizabeth Wood and Mr. Philip Pearce on behalf of Thomas Beckford Esq. to serve Mr. Peter Furnell of Kingston, Jamaica.

William Tuffe, baptised 24 December 1741, son of William T., admitted from Whitchurch Canonicorum, Dorset, by order of Court; 29 January 1757 to his friend John Tuffe Esq. to serve Mr. George Savage of Antigua, merchant.

Admissions in April 1749

Robert Duport, baptised 13 March 1740, son of John D., admitted from Barking, Essex; 27 January 1755 to Mr. George Sussex of Tooley Street, Southwark, to serve his father George Sussex Sr. in Halifax, Nova Scotia.

John Vinicombe, baptised 5 July 1738, son of John V., baker, admitted from St. Dunstan Stepney; 8 January 1754 to his mother Mary V. and Mr. Archibald Darrack of London, mariner, to serve Thomas Lessly Esq. of Antigua, merchant.

James Beech, baptised 17 December 1738, son of Richard B., vintner, admitted from St. Alkmond, Shrewsbury, Shropshire; 23 September 1754 to his sister Mary B. and Alexander Grant, merchant, to serve Major-General Charles Dawes of Jamaica, merchant.

Robert Carvel, baptised 8 October 1738, son of William C., admitted from Haselbech, Northamptonshire; 1 June 1754 to Andrew Lessly, Mr. of the *Bassnett* bound for Antigua.

Stephen Rose, baptised 22 January 1741, son of Thomas R., weaver, admitted from St. Bride's; 25 February 1755 to his uncle John Landman and Richard Oliver of London, merchant, to serve Mr. Daniel Warner of Antigua, merchant.

George Littleton, baptised 17 July 1743, son of Charles L., admitted from St. Mary Woolnoth; 20 January 1759 to Alexander Hamilton, Mr. of the *Peak Bay* bound for Jamaica.

Joseph Henry Huddleston, baptised 9 November 1740, son of Rev. William H., admitted from Newenden, Kent; 9 September 1755 to his sister Mary H. on behalf of his mother Frances H. of Bromley, Kent, and to Mr. John Stiles to serve his brother Mr. Copeland Stiles in Barbados, merchant.

Benjamin Raffles, baptised 29 July 1739, son of Thomas R., admitted from St. Ann Blackfriars; 12 July 1755 to George Hooper, Mr. of the *Martin* bound for Antigua.

Admissions in April 1750

Joseph Mead, born 15 September 1742, son of John M., clothworker, admitted from St. Michael Crooked Lane; 8 September 1757 to his mother Elizabeth M. to serve George Johnson, Mr. of the *Annandale* bound for Carolina.

Thomas Watton, baptised 6 September 1741, son of Thomas W., framework knitter, admitted from St. Ann, Middlesex; 4 August 1756 to his uncle John W. and Beeston Long, merchant, to serve William Gale Esq. of Jamaica, planter.

William Portsmouth, baptised 23 November 1740, son of William P., cordwainer, admitted from St. Stephen Coleman Street; 14 July 1756 to Daniel Curling to serve George Curling, Mr. of the *Prince of Wales* bound for Carolina.

John Delves, baptised 28 May 1736, son of Hugh D., admitted from St. James Westminster; 30 June 1752 to his aunt — Page and Mr. Marmaduke Hilton of London, merchant, to serve Mr. Aaron Manby of Kingstown, Jamaica, ironmonger.

Francis Harrison, baptised 27 November 1742, son of John H., innholder, admitted from St. Lawrence Jewry; 18 February 1758 to Robert Manley, Mr. of the *New Elizabeth* bound for Barbados.

Adam Barlow, baptised 4 September 1741, son of Adam B., admitted from St. Michael Cornhill; 11 October 1756 to his mother Dinah B. and Mr. Stephen Venn of Mark Lane, merchant, to serve Rev. John Venny of Spanish Town, Jamaica.

William Palmer, baptised 2 December 1740, son of Samuel P., admitted from St. Andrew Holborn in the place of Robert Adcock; 25 September 1755 to his friend Mr. Charles Green of Bridge Street, Westminster, and Henry Brouncker Esq., Collector of Customs at St. Christopher's, to serve Martin Manning, merchant, in St. Christopher's.

Admissions in April 1751

Edward Bingley, baptised 7 October 1743, son of William B., free waterman, admitted from St. Mary Whitechapel; 14 September 175? to his aunt Sarah Applewhite to serve Robert Smith, Mr. of the *Thames* bound for Boston, New England.

John Lewis, baptised 16 August 1744, son of John L., musician, admitted from St. Sepulchre; 19 March 1759 to his mother Susan Bowles and Mr. Benjamin Gerrish to serve Joseph Gerrish Esq., Naval Storekeeper and merchant in Halifax, Nova Scotia.

Charles Doughty, baptised 24 November 1743, son of Charles D., admitted from St. James Westminster; 28 June 1760 to Neal Maxwell, Mr. of the *Crown* bound for St. Christopher's.

William Bush, baptised 11 September 1741, son of Robert B., carpenter, admitted from St. Botolph Bishopsgate; 1 April 1757 to his aunt Elizabeth B. and Beeston Long, merchant, to serve James Dawkins Esq. of Jamaica, planter.

George William Freeman, baptised 16 February 1743, son of Edwin F., skinner, admitted from St. Peter Paul's Wharf in the place of William Savage; 20 October 1757 to his mother Mary F. to serve Mr. John Watkins, attorney at law in Antigua.

Abraham Riley, born 12 May 1744, son of Daniel R., admitted from St. James Clerkenwell; 9 August 1759 to his said father to serve William Smith, Mr. of the *William* bound for New York.

John Marsh, baptised 29 July 1743, son of John M., admitted from Newbury, Berkshire, in the place of Joseph Cooper; 30 August 1758 to his said father to serve James Nevin Esq., Collector of Customs at Piscataqua, New England.

John Lacy Hawkins, baptised 14 October 1744, son of Payne H., painter stainer, admitted from St. Mary Magdalen Old Fish Street; 31 January 1761 to David Ochterlony, Mr. of the *Olive* bound for New York.

Admissions in April 1753

Thomas Edward Reade, baptised 28 April 1745, son of Philip Edward R., distiller, admitted from St. Austin; 20 January 1759 to George Curling, Mr. of the *Prince of Wales* bound for Carolina.

Thomas Frazer, baptised 19 September 1742, son of Peter F., admitted from St. James Westminster; 21 October 1757 to his mother Elizabeth F. and Mr. Richard Maitland to serve Mr. Anthony Wharton of St. Christopher's, merchant.

Isaac William Crouch, baptised 5 August 1744, son of Edward C., admitted from St. Andrew Holborn; 24 November 1759 to Samuel Ball, Mr. of the *Friendship* bound for South Carolina.

William Maud, born 1 October 1743, son of William M., admitted from St. Dunstan in the West; 4 November 1757 to R. March on behalf of the boy's grandmother and Mr. Thomas Smith of St. Paul's Churchyard, merchant, to serve

Lawrence Irvine, Mr. of the *Lyon* bound for Jamaica.

William Langford, baptised 28 September 1746, son of Edward L., glover, admitted from St. Bartholomew the Less; 5 November 1763 to Samuel Hardy, Mr. of the *Dorsetshire* bound for St. Kitts.

Charles Dixon, baptised 3 November 1745, son of Charles D., plasterer, admitted from St. Michael Bassishaw; 11 September 1762 to James Millar, Mr. of the *Brilliant* bound for Jamaica.

Henry Pope, baptised 22 December 1745, son of William P., admitted from Sherborne, Dorset, in the place of Robert Simmonds; 13 February 1762 to John Smith, Mr. of the *Elizabeth* bound for Antigua.

Admissions in April 1755

Charles Tomkins, baptised 19 May 1747, son of John T., tiler and bricklayer, admitted from St. Stephen Coleman Street; 21 March 1762 to his mother Jane T. to serve Captain John Smith of Princes Street, Royal Exchange, merchant, in Antigua.

John Wheeler, baptised 3 January 1745, son of Rev. James W., admitted from Maidwell, Northamptonshire; 9 November 1759 to Hannah Wheeler and Mr. Beeston Long, merchant, to serve Hon. Henry Dawkins of Jamaica, planter.

John Spencer, born 13 May 1746, son of John S., wheelwright, admitted from St. Sepulchre; 3 November 1760 to his father-in-law William Selby and Mr. John Piggott of London, merchant, to serve William Hall of Bermuda, merchant.

Israel Johannot, baptised 5 July 1744, son of Josias J., stationer, admitted from All Hallows Lombard Street; 20 January 1759 to Rowland Crisp, Mr. of the *Countess of Effingham* bound for Jamaica.

Thomas Burton, born 2 March 1747, son of John B., admitted from Croydon, Surrey; 9 October 1762 to Timothy

Mangles, Mr. of the galley *Genoa* bound for Lisbon and the West Indies.

John Simpson, born 18 March 1747, son of David S., admitted from St. Martin in the Fields; 4 October 1760 to his mother Katherine S. to serve Henry Dawkins Esq. of Jamaica, merchant.

Samuel Mansell, baptised 26 October 1748, son of Godfrey M., admitted from the Liberty of the Old Artillery Ground; 23 May 1764 to Richard Budden, Mr. of the *Philadelphia Packet* bound for Philadelphia.

John Keble, baptised 22 August 1744, son of Thomas K., painter stainer, admitted from St. Botolph Bishopsgate; 22 March 1759 to Edward Welch and Mr. James Aiskell to serve Thomas Penn Esq., Proprietor of Pennsylvania.

John Tannatt, baptised in May 1747, son of Thomas T., admitted from Oswestry, Shropshire; 18 January 1762 to Mr. Robert Pott of London, merchant, to serve Thomas Storer Esq. of Jamaica, merchant.

William Brown, born 30 September 1743, son of Richard B., admitted from St. James Westminster; 26 August 1758 to Andrew Lessly, Mr. of the *Bassnett* bound for Antigua.

David La Verge, baptised 15 February 1746, son of Daniel La V., admitted from St. Leonard Shoreditch; 3 October 1760 to his uncle Thomas King living at the *Shakespeare's Head* in Moorfields and Mr. Beeston Long, merchant, to serve Henry Dawkins Esq. of Jamaica, merchant.

Matthias Hathaway, baptised 1 May 1746, son of Rev. Paul H., admitted from St. Ann Westminster; 7 January 1761 to Mr. George Farr, grocer of Newgate Street, on behalf of the mother, to serve Mr. Benjamin Davis, merchant of Boston, New England.

Admissions in April 1756

John Boreman, baptised 28 February 1748, son of John B., carpenter, admitted from St. Botolph Aldgate; 11 October

1762 to his first cousin Mrs. Ann Brown and Mr. John Strettell of London, merchant, to serve Mr. Amos Strettell of Philadelphia, merchant.

Henry Bull, baptised 7 November 1750, son of Thomas B., mason, admitted from St. Peter le Poor; 26 February 1765 to his uncle-in-law Mr. William Gardner to serve Mr. Nathaniel Bird of Newport, Rhode Island, merchant.

William Mansfield, baptised 1 February 1748, son of Benjamin M., haberdasher, admitted from St. Peter Cornhill; 16 September 1762 to his aunt Catherine Ombles of Leadenhall Market and Mr. Charles Crockatt of London, merchant, to serve Thomas Boone Esq., Governor of South Carolina.

Thomas Hamson, baptised 9 February 1748, son of Thomas H., admitted from St. George the Martyr, Middlesex; 23 November 1762 to his said father to serve Mr. John Harvey of Antigua, planter.

Brummit Julian, baptised 6 May 1748, son of Bramman J., admitted from St. George the Martyr, Middlesex; 24 October 1764 to Alexander Hamilton, Mr. of the *Jamaica* bound for Jamaica.

William Shayler, baptised 27 January 1749, son of Robert S., admitted from East Greenwich, Kent; 22 February 1764 to Howard Jacobs, Mr. of the *Boscawen* bound for New England.

James Elliot, baptised 19 January 1746, son of James E., stationer, admitted from St. Clement Danes; 5 November 1763 to Roderick Wilson, Mr. of the *Prince of Wales* bound for Antigua.

Samuel Ashley, baptised 30 November 1747, son of John A., weaver, admitted from St. Luke, Middlesex; 1 December 1762 to his uncle Edward A. of New John Street, Grays Inn Lane, to serve Mr. Edward Foord of Kingston, Jamaica, merchant.

Henry Wheeler, baptised 18 May 1745, son of Henry W.,

carpenter, admitted from St. Martin Vintry; 17 February 1761 to Benjamin Bell, Mr. of the *Two Sisters* bound for Virginia.

Noy Willey Hutchins, baptised 10 January 1748, son of John H., fishmonger, admitted from St. Margaret New Fish Street; 15 October 1762 to his mother Sarah H. to serve Mr. George Parker of Charles Town, South Carolina, merchant.

John Young, baptised 27 December 1745, son of Philip Y., admitted from South Weald, Essex; 9 October 1762 to George Young, Mr. of the *Martinique* bound for the West Indies.

John Sibley, baptised 11 December 1748, son of Stephen S., admitted from Hampstead, Middlesex; 18 March 1763 to his said father and Charles Dingley Esq. of Lothbury, merchant, to serve Mr. Mark Hall of Jamaica, planter.

Daniel Clark, baptised 12 December 1745, son of Thomas C., admitted from St. Mary le Bow; 27 October 1760 to his said father of Bow Lane, Cheapside, to serve Mr. Bond, merchant of Jamaica.

William Dibon, baptised 19 November 1747, son of William D., blacksmith, admitted from St. Martin Ironmonger Lane in the place of William Crabb; 2 January 1762 to his friend Mrs. Mary Bradley of Kensington to serve Edward Morant Esq. of Clarendon, Jamaica, merchant.

Admissions in April 1757

Matthew Hutchins, baptised 10 December 1747, son of William H., admitted from St. Ann Westminster; 19 October 1762 to his said father of Oxford Road and Mr. Henry Rainsdon on behalf of Mr. Jonathan Bernard of London, merchant, to serve Mr. George Irving, merchant, in Boston, New England.

Benjamin Parker, born 24 May 1747, son of George P., haberdasher, admitted from St. Dionis Backchurch; 12 October 1761 to his mother Sarah P. to serve Mr. Matthew

Grave of Kingston, Jamaica, merchant.

Thomas Peplow, baptised 17 July 1748, son of John P., admitted from Wentnor, Shropshire; 8 March 1763 with the consent of his said father to serve Robert Holden of Jamaica, merchant. [Letter from the father dated Shrewsbury 25 February 1763 asking for his son's discharge].

Edward Churchill, baptised 6 November 1749, son of Samuel C., baker, admitted from St. Sepulchre; 15 March 1764 to his mother Ann C. and Benjamin Boddington of London, merchant, to serve Ann Freeman of Antigua, planter.

Thomas Roker, baptised 21 June 1747, son of Philip R., goldsmith, admitted from East Greenwich, Kent; 22 September 1761 to his mother Elizabeth R. to serve James Furlong of Antigua, merchant.

William Banks, baptised 18 April 1750, son of Richard B., admitted from St. Bartholomew the Less; 20 May 1767 to James Jeffries, Mr. of the *Britannia* bound for Philadelphia.

Thomas Gibbons, baptised 4 May 1750, son of Matthew G., goldsmith, admitted from St. Andrew Holborn; 15 May 1764 to his said father of Chapel Street, Tottenham Court Road, and Mr. Richard Drakeford of Queen Street, merchant, to serve Mr. William Wilkinson of Bermuda.

William Ryley, born 28 April 1746, son of Samuel R., stationer, admitted from St. Dunstan in the West; 29 August 1761 to Thomas Mapstone, Mr. of the *Friendship* bound for Barbados.

Richard Barnard, baptised 22 January 1750, son of Richard B., musician, admitted from St. Michael Cornhill; 18 May 1765 to his uncle Mr. John Griffiths of Lombard Street, woollen draper, to serve Richard Wayne of Charles Town, South Carolina, merchant.

John Smith, baptised 14 February 1748, son of Thomas S., upholder, admitted from Earls Colne, Essez; 28 November 1762 to his friend Mr. James Gibbs, watchmaker of Fetter

Lane, and Mr. Thomas Raffles of Doctors Commons to serve his son Mr. Thomas Raffles of Port Morant, Jamaica, merchant.

Anthony Narroway, baptised 17 December 1749, son of George N., weaver, admitted from St. Botolph Bishopsgate; 2 June 1764 to his brother James N. to serve Mr. William Allen, merchant of Golden Square, Chief Justice of Pennsylvania.

Samuel Clark, baptised 20 January 1749, son of Thomas C., admitted from St. Mary le Bow; 15 June 1763 to Samuel Bull, Mr. of the *Britannia* bound for Jamaica.

David Crook, baptised 17 December 1746, son of Jonathan C., admitted from St. John Wapping, presented by the parish of St. Mary Whitechapel, in the place of Samuel Hawkins; 2 December 1760 to his brother Jonathan C. and Mr. Samuel Turner of London, merchant, to serve John Dunn of Antigua, merchant.

Edward Moss, baptised 30 December 1748, son of Charles M., clothworker, admitted from St. Stephen Coleman Street in the place of Cornelius Ketteral; 9 March 1763 to his mother Margaret M. to serve Thomas Foster of St. Elizabeth, Jamaica, merchant.

William Wiseham, baptised 14 October 1749, son of Samuel W., fishmonger, admitted from All Hallows Lombard Street in the place of Sarah Pearse; 31 January 1765 to his said father and Mr. Richard Yates to serve Mr. Lawrence Reade of New York, merchant.

James Tollman, baptised 24 September 1745, son of James T., cook, admitted from St. Andrew Hubbard in the place of Henry White; 29 August 1761 to Charles Robinson, Mr. of the *Manning* bound for Jamaica.

Admissions in April 1758

William Neate, baptised 3 June 1752, son of Thomas N., carpenter, admitted from St. Alban Wood Street; 11 March 1767 to Mr. Thomas Fraser of Nicholas Lane, merchant, to serve Mr. James Fraser of Barbados, merchant.

John Staplin, baptised 11 May 1748, son of Rev. William S., admitted from Tiverton, Devon; 18 November 1762 to his cousin Mr. Francis Dalby of Orchard Street, Westminster, merchant, and Richard Oliver Esq. of Golden Square, merchant, to serve James Athill of Antigua, surgeon and apothecary.

Jacob May, baptised 17 February 1750, son of John M., admitted from St. Mary Islington; 28 November 1764 to his mother Ann M. to serve Foster Barham Esq. of Jamaica, planter.

John Hudson, baptised 26 March 1750, son of Edmond H., admitted from Banstead, Surrey; 26 June 1764 to his mother Elizabeth H. of Banstead to serve William Allen Esq., Chief Justice of Pennsylvania.

William Woodards, baptised 29 March 1752, son of Thomas W., farrier, admitted from St. Andrew Holborn by order of Court; 7 November 1766 to his mother Rebecca Hall to serve Edward Clarke Esq. of Montego Bay, Jamaica, planter.

Benjamin Sawyer, baptised 12 May 1747, son of Benjamin S., wheelwright, admitted from St. Gregory by St. Paul; 28 January 1762 to his mother Mary Watson to serve Mr. Peter Brotherson of St. Christopher's, merchant.

Joseph Preston, baptised 10 June 1753, son of William P., carpenter, admitted from St. John Hackney; 2 September 1767 to his mother Ann P. to serve Joseph Sherburne of Boston, New England, merchant.

John Speck, baptised 6 January 1751, son of John S., carman, admitted from St. Leonard Shoreditch; 12 March 1766 to his mother Elizabeth S. to serve John Harvey Esq. of Grenada, merchant.

Richard Bright Winslow, baptised 31 May 1752, son of Richard W., cooper, admitted from St. Katherine Creechurch; 7 November 1766 to his mother Catherine W. to serve

Edward Clarke Esq. of Montego Bay, Jamaica.

Richard Davies, baptised 28 January 1752, son of Rev. Thomas D. admitted from Ystraddyfodwg, Glamorgan; 30 June 1767 with the consent of his mother Ann D. to James Brebner Esq. of Antigua, merchant.

John Flameng, baptised 7 May 1749, son of John F., grocer, admitted from St. Katherine Creechurch; 16 June 1764 to Leslie Groves, Mr. of the *Hillsborough* bound for the West Indies.

Joseph Mascall, born 7 November 1753, son of Joseph M., vintner, admitted from St. Bartholomew by the Exchange; 17 November 1770 to Walter Brett, Mr. of the *Judith Hillaria* bound for Jamaica.

Benjamin Jones, baptised 5 February 1750, son of Evan Jones, admitted from St. Luke, Middlesex, in the place of William King; 20 July 1765 to Thomas Adams, Mr. of the *Sincere Friend* bound for Barbados.

James Hickman, born 18 December 1750, son of John H., fanmaker, admitted from St. Michael Bassishaw in the place of Joseph Hickman; 3 May 1765 to his mother Hannah H. and William Daling of London, merchant, to serve James Shepherd of Barbados, planter.

James Riley, born 22 November 1748, son of James R., admitted from St. James Clerkenwell; 28 November 1763 to his uncle Mr. Daniel R. to serve Thomas Foster Esq. of Upper Brook Street, Grosvenor Square, as a planter in Jamaica.

James Creed, baptised 19 November 1750, son of Edward C., admitted from St. Lawrence, Reading, Berkshire; 26 February 1765 to William Charles on behalf of the boy's friend Thomas Clarke, gunsmith of Fetter Lane, to serve Mr. Nathaniel Bird of Newport, Rhode Island, merchant.

Admissions in April 1759

Charles Norwood, baptised 17 June 1753, son of Charles N., barber surgeon, admitted from St. Andrew Hubbard; 2 June 1770 to John Waugh, Mr. of the *British King* bound for the West Indies.

John Splatt Cripps, baptised 5 April 1754, son of William C., girdler, admitted from St. Bartholomew the Less; 29 July 1768 to his father-in-law Mr. Alexander Gillen of Charles Town, South Carolina, merchant.

William Ferriman, baptised 9 January 1750, son of Joseph F., wheelwright, admitted from St. Botolph Bishopsgate; 28 January 1766 to his said father of Mile End and Mr. Thomas Lane of London, merchant, to serve Mr. William Pitman of Salem, New England.

Thomas Goldwin, baptised 24 September 1749, son of John G., admitted from New Windsor, Berkshire; 28 November 1763 to his sister Christian G. and Mr. Beeston Long, merchant, to serve Edward Long Esq. of Jamaica, planter.

William Belany, baptised 29 September 1751, son of William B., cordwainer, admitted from St. Andrew Holborn; 7 May 1768 to Henry Brand Jr., Mr. of the *Juno* bound for Newfoundland.

Henry Glover, baptised 7 April 1751, son of Henry G., coachmaker, admitted from All Hallows on the Wall; 10 October 1765 to his half-brother William Knewstub, cutler of Antigua.

Thomas Ann Clarke, baptised 20 October 1754, son of Rev. James C., admitted from St. Mary le Strand; 6 August 1768 to his said father to serve Fenwick Bull of Charles Town, South Carolina, attorney at law.

William Burt, born in February 1750, son of John B., farrier, admitted from St. Sepulchre; 14 March 1765 to his mother Susannah B. and Mr. Robert Latimer on behalf of Isaac King of London, merchant, to serve Samuel Perroneau Esq. of South Carolina, merchant.

William Augustus Skynner, baptised 22 October 1748, son of

William S., clothworker, admitted from St. Michael Wood Street; 5 November 1763 to James Hume, Mr. of the *Hawke* bound for Antigua.

Thomas Tatler, baptised 18 June 1750, son of Thomas T., admitted from St. Saviour Southwark; 20 July 1765 to Richard Budden, Mr. of the *Philadelphia Packet* bound for Philadelphia.

John Dongworth, baptised 15 October 1749, son of William D., innholder, admitted from St. Mary Aldermanbury; 18 June 1764 to Charles Wilson, Mr. of the *Hawke* bound for the West Indies.

William Tapp, baptised 3 December 1749, son of Lavington T., wheelwright, admitted from Christ Church; 3 August 1764 with the consent of his mother Jane T. of Normanton, Nottinghamshire, to his cousin Mr. John Simons and Captain Christian Jacobson to serve Mr. William Hawkshurst of New York, merchant.

Clayton Haines Littlehales, baptised 9 December 1750, son of John L., admitted from St. George Hanover Square; 23 November 1764 to his mother Shepherdess L. and George Drake Esq. of London, merchant, to serve William Fowler Esq. of Jamaica, planter.

Thomas Powell, baptised 24 April 1752, son of Thomas P., admitted from Kington, Herefordshire; 2 May 1766 to his mother Milborough P. and George Drake Esq., merchant, to serve William Gale of Jamaica, planter.

William Bockham, baptised 3 May 1752, son of Oliver B., founder, admitted from All Hallows the Less; 14 November 1769 to his mother Mary Williams to serve Hesketh Davis, Mr. of the *Britannia* bound for Barbados.

John Burnett, baptised 1 January 1750, son of Robert B., admitted from St. Margaret Pattens; 13 December 1764 to his mother Elizabeth B. and Mr. James Haymers to serve Peregrine Cust Esq. of London, merchant, in New York or [?New] England.

Thomas Spackman, baptised 20 March 1748, son of Benjamin S., embroiderer, admitted from St. Margaret Lothbury; 12 November 1762 to his mother Elizabeth S. to serve Mrs. Martha Bargeau of St. David's, Jamaica, merchant.

Daniel Horne, baptised 28 May 1749, son of William H., butcher, admitted from St. Faith under St. Paul's; 6 December 1766 to Thomas Blackburn, Mr. of the *Harriott* bound for Barbados.

William Allsop, baptised 24 March 1751, son of John A., feltmaker, admitted from St. John Southwark; 17 July 1765 to Roderick Wilson, Mr. of the *Prince of Wales* bound for the West Indies.

John Smith, baptised 2 December 1750, son of John S., blacksmith, admitted from St. Michael Crooked Lane; 3 May 1765 to his said father and Mr. William Daling, merchant, to serve James Shepherd of Barbados, planter.

Thomas Riley, baptised 3 July 1750, son of James R., admitted from St. James Clerkenwell; 20 February 1765 to Grizell Haigh and John White of Hyde Street, Bloomsbury, to serve William White of St. Ann's, Jamaica, merchant.

Robert Rosindall, baptised 4 January 1753, son of John R., admitted from Barking, Essex, in the place of William Wright; 25 November 1765 to Benjamin Hughes, Mr. of the *Augustus Caesar* bound for Jamaica.

Admissions in April 1760

Richard Rutland, baptised 10 May 1750, son of Richard R., admitted from Hopton Wafers, Shropshire; 22 April 1765 to his said father to serve Roger Hope Elletson Esq. of Curzon Street, Mayfair, as a planter in Jamaica.

Henry Wedmore Perry, baptised 4 October 1751, son of Francis P., admitted from Portsea, Hampshire, by order of Court; 10 March 1766 to his mother Sarah Ashfield to serve Mr. Richard Yates of New York, merchant.

William Bradshaw, baptised 26 August 1750, son of John B., admitted from St. Saviour Southwark; 23 April 1766 to Robert Mirrie, Mr. of the *Simmond* bound for the West Indies.

James Rosseter, baptised 3 March 1751, son of James R., admitted from St. Olave Southwark; 29 January 1766 to George Anderson, Mr. of the *Savannah Packet* bound for Georgia.

Aminadab Peck, baptised 31 August 1753, son of John P., admitted from St. Botolph Aldersgate; 26 May 1770 to Richard Neale, Mr. of the galley *Redhead* bound for the West Indies.

William Monksfield, baptised 30 August 1749, son of William M., admitted from St. George the Martyr, Middlesex; 5 June 1764 to his mother Mary M. to serve Thomas Penn Esq., Proprietor of Pennsylvania.

John Harper, baptised 14 May 1750, son of John H., admitted from Chilton Foliatt, Wiltshire; 23 November 1765 to John Defell, Mr. of the *Augustus Caesar* bound for Jamaica.

John Richardson, baptised 10 March 1754, son of James R., admitted from Hadleigh, Suffolk; 13 April 1769 to his brother-in-law Mr. John White on behalf of his mother Elizabeth R. of Haw Park near Ipswich, to serve Charles Spooner Esq. of South Audley Street, as a planter at St. Christopher's.

William Selwood, baptised 29 September 1751, son of William S., admitted from St. Lawrence, Exeter, Devon; 25 November 1766 to John Gignoux of Watling Street, merchant, to serve Mrs. Ann Freeman of Antigua, planter.

Charles Knapton, baptised 31 March 1753, son of Walter K., admitted from Ilston, Leicestershire; 14 December 1767 with the consent of his mother Mary K. of Northampton to serve Mr. Dottin Battyn of London, merchant, in Barbados.

Joseph Yates, born 4 November 1753, son of William Y., admitted from St. Sepulchre; 19 February 1768 to his said father of Durham Yard, Smithfield, to serve Mr. Delacourt Walsh of Antigua, planter.

Robert Creed, baptised 13 July 1752, son of Edward C., admitted from St. Lawrence, Reading, Berkshire; 26 May 1767 with the consent of his uncle James Bestbridge of Reading to Thomas Walker Esq. of Soho Square to serve him in Barbados.

John Woodin, baptised 10 May 1750, son of Henry W., barber surgeon, admitted from St. Ann Blackfriars in the place of Michael Abbot; 10 July 1765 to Benjamin Raffles, Mr. of the *Morant* bound for Jamaica.

James Tomes, born 1 February 1753, son of John T., admitted from Newbury, Berkshire, in the place of Benjamin Tomes; 27 June 1767 to his brother Benjamin T. to serve Robert Maitland Esq. of Antigua. [Benjamin Tomes, listed as son of *Joseph* T., was admitted in 1756 and discharged to go to Madeira in June 1761].

Admissions in March 1762

Joseph Snape, baptised 17 June 1753, son of Robert S., framework knitter, admitted from St. Leonard Shoreditch; 20 October 1767 to his said father and George Drake, merchant, to serve Henry Dawkins Esq. of Clarendon, Jamaica.

John Lawes, born 10 November 1755, son of John L., cordwainer, admitted from St. Lawrence Jewry; 6 November 1770 to Josiah Howard of Mile End Old Town to serve Mr. George Moulton of St. Dorothy's, Jamaica, merchant.

Edward Southcombe, baptised 15 July 1753, son of Angel S., admitted from St. James Westminster; 15 December 1769 to his uncle-in-law Francis Edward Vallotton of Queen Street, Seven Dials, to serve Benjamin Raffles, Mr. of the *Caesar* bound for Jamaica.

Thomas Whittle Bear, baptised 5 March 1752, son of Thomas B., admitted from Bulmer, Essex; 7 November 1766 to Mr. Henry Wells, butcher of St. James Market on behalf of the uncle, Mr. John Whittle of Barton [*?Barcombe*], Sussex, to serve Mr. William Redhead of Antigua, apothecary and surgeon.

William Ingram, baptised 20 January 1754, son of Hastings I., fishmonger, admitted from St. Dunstan Stepney; 13 October 1770 to James Moore, Mr. of the *Trecothick* bound for Grenada.

Joseph Burchett, baptised 11 September 1750, son of William B., stationer, admitted from Whitefriars Precinct; 3 September 1765 to his said father to serve Mr. William Dickinson of Antigua, merchant.

Thomas Stocker, baptised 18 March 1753, son of Abraham S., free waterman, admitted from Christ Church Southwark; 27 July 1768 to his mother Mary S. and Richard Oliver, merchant, to serve William Thomas Esq. of Antigua, planter.

Admissions in March 1763

John Garrett, born 17 July 1756, son of John G., glass seller, admitted from St. Augustine; 5 June 1771 to his aunt Sarah Walklate of Aldersgate Street to serve Mr. Abraham Constable, master shipwright of His Majesty's Yard at Halifax, Nova Scotia.

Edmund Squire, baptised 13 September 1753, son of Rev. John S., admitted from Lavenham, Suffolk; 9 February 1768 with the consent of his mother Ann S. to Samuel Beachcroft Esq. of London, merchant, to serve Lord Olyphand in Jamaica.

Edward Crouch, baptised 29 October 1752, son of Joseph C., joiner, admitted from St. Antholin; 27 October 1766 to his said father to serve Mr. Robert Holden of Kingston, Jamaica, merchant.

George Matthews, baptised 2 September 1755, son of Thomas M., loriner, admitted from St. Sepulchre; 3 June 1772 to Samuel Ball Jr., Mr. of the *Britannia* bound for Carolina.

Henry Russell, baptised 21 October 1753, son of Robert R., admitted from St. Martin in the Fields; 12 February 1768 to his said father to serve Thomas Walker Esq. of Soho Square in Jamaica.

Isaac Baker, baptised 13 March 1754, son of Charles Bowles Baker who omitted to take up the freedom of the City of London although entitled, admitted from St. Michael Crooked Lane by order of Court; 28 July 1768 to his aunt Ann Payne of Bow Lane and Richard Oliver Esq., merchant, to serve William Thomas Esq. of Antigua.

John Clay, baptised 21 November 1756, son of John C., musician, admitted from St. Ethelburga Bishopsgate; 27 February 1771 to his brother William C. and Mr. James Bayle French of Wood Street to serve Mr. William Dottin of Barbados, planter.

Thomas Yates, born 23 August and baptised 7 September 1755, son of William Y., admitted from St. Sepulchre; 8 August 1770 to his said father of Smithfield to serve Mr. Gibbs, merchant of Charles Town, South Carolina.

William Blakemore, baptised 16 April 1752, son of Thomas B., admitted from Rodington, Shropshire, by special order of Court; 19 February 1768 with the consent of his friend Mrs. Elizabeth Bosanquet to John Pinchbeck to serve Mr. Delacourt Walsh of Antigua, merchant.

Admissions in March 1764

John Maddox, baptised 5 January 1758, son of Robert M., innholder, admitted from St. Sepulchre; 13 November 1773 to John Brewer, Mr. of the *Manning* bound for Jamaica.

George Lobb, baptised 3 December 1756, son of George L., tinplate worker, admitted from St. Olave Southwark;

27 February 1771 to his said father to serve Mr. John Bland of Lime Street, merchant, in Virginia.

Henry Hardy, baptised 5 November 1754, son of John H., admitted from Liverpool, Lancashire; 15 May 1771 to James Holmes, Mr. of the *Loyal Briton* bound for Grenada.

William Timothy Seaman, baptised 10 October 1755, son of Timothy S., pewterer, admitted from St. Peter Cornhill; 18 December 1769 to his grandmother Mrs. Mary Lowe of Leadenhall Market and Mr. John Read of Queen Street, Cheapside, to serve Mr. Henry Topham, Naval Officer of Antigua.

George Wright Knowles, baptised 24 June 1754, son of Rev. William K., admitted from Thetford St. Mary, Suffolk; 4 February 1769 at the request of his mother Susannah K. of Thetford to his cousin John Fawles, attorney of Old Buildings, Lincolns Inn, to serve Mr. John Stenhouse, merchant of Montreal, Quebec.

Admissions in March 1765

William Ward Farrer, baptised 8 July 1759, son of William F., wheelwright, admitted from St. Benet Sherehog; 4 February 1775 to Simon Lee, Mr. of the *Polly & Charlotte* bound for Madeira and Barbados.

James Corp, baptised 2 November 1754, son of Samuel C., cordwainer, admitted from St. Clement Danes; 22 December 1769 to his said father and Ninian Ballantine of Wood Street, druggist, to serve William Redhead of Parham, Antigua, surgeon and apothecary.

John Houchins, baptised 18 June 1758, son of Samuel H., cooper, admitted from Low Layton, Essex; 12 January 1773 to his brother James H., cooper of Leytonstone, Essex, to serve Valentine Morris Esq. of St. Vincent upon his estate in Antigua.

Bateman Baker, baptised 27 April 1755, son of Charles Bowles B., admitted from St. Michael Crooked Lane; 18 May 1771 to Henry Mowat, commander of the *Canceaux* bound for Nova Scotia.

James Bridge, baptised 20 June 1756, son of Thomas B., admitted from St. Faith the Virgin; 22 April 1771 to his sister Martha B. of Grocers' Hall, Poultry, to serve Main Swete Walrond Esq. of Antigua, planter.

John Bull Mathison, born in December 1756, son of Richard M., admitted from St. Margaret Lothbury; 3 November 1773 to Phillip Millar, Mr. of the *Charming Nelly* bound for Jamaica.

John Birch, baptised 12 March 1758, son of John B., admitted from St. Ann Westminster; 30 October 1773 to Robert Curling, Mr. of the *Beckford* bound for Jamaica.

Charles Gander, baptised 22 May 1755, son of John G., admitted from Sherborne, Dorset, in the place of James Gander; 26 October 1772 to his brother John G. of New Street, Covent Garden, to serve William Magness, Mr. of the *Ann & Elizabeth* bound for Jamaica. [*His brother James Gander, baptised in July 1751, was apprenticed in 1765 to a stationer in Sherborne*].

Robert Stevens, baptised 13 September 1758, son of Robert S., tinplate worker, admitted from St. James Garlickhithe in the place of Thomas Park; 10 December 1774 to William Magness, Mr. of the *Ann & Elizabeth* bound for Jamaica.

John Sedgwick, baptised 11 February 1753, son of Robert S., admitted from St. Stephen Coleman Street in the place of James Siddall Walter; 19 May 1770 to Joseph Judge, Mr. of the *Elizabeth* bound for Quebec.

Admissions in March 1766

James Terry, baptised 1 May 1758, son of Garnett T., carpenter; 5 January 1773 to his mother Frances Agar and William Thomson, merchant of New Court, Throckmorton Street, to serve James Leslie of Spanish Town, Jamaica, attorney at law.

Charles Ashley, baptised 13 April 1755, son of Edward A., barber, admitted from St. Andrew Holborn; 31 July 1769 to his said father of Baldwin Gardens, New Leather Lane, to serve Mr. John Bland of Lime Street, merchant, in Virginia.

William Ward, baptised 22 May 1757, son of William W., feltmaker, admitted from St. George in the East, Middlesex; 15 May 1773 to John Kilty, Mr. of the *Polly* bound for Maryland.

Samuel Frances, baptised 7 November 1756, son of William F., admitted from Lamport, Northamptonshire; 14 August 1771 to his brother William F. on behalf of his said father to serve Barlow Trecothick Esq., merchant and alderman of London, on his estate in Jamaica.

Stephen Newton Livesey, born 5 August 1761, son of George L., admitted from Walsall, Staffordshire; 13 November 1777 to William Hore, Mr. of the *Mary* bound for Jamaica.

William Jones, born 31 October 1757, son of John J., admitted from Bethnal Green; 29 April 1772 to Roberts Necks, Mr. of the *Lunn & Lloyd* bound for Virginia.

George Shield, baptised 27 June 1757, son of Rev. Benjamin S., admitted from Sible Hedingham, Essex; 28 June 1775 to Henry Wilson, Mr. of the *Adamant* bound for Quebec.

William Jordan, baptised 17 August 1755, son of William J., goldsmith, admitted from Sandwich, Kent; 2 November 1769 with the consent of his said father to Harry Smith Esq., Collector of Customs of St. Vincent.

Richard Bate, baptised 7 November 1755, son of Rev. Henry B., admitted from Chelmsford, Essex; 27 January 1770 to his brother Rev. Henry B. on behalf of his said father to serve Mr. John Bland of Lime Street, merchant, in Virginia.

Robert Huggins, baptised 7 February 1757, son of Edward H., admitted from St. Lawrence, Reading, Berkshire, in the place of Benjamin Wright; 4 February 1771 with the consent of his said father to Mr. James Grossett of Little Newport Street to serve James Burnett Esq., Naval Storekeeper in Jamaica.

Admissions in March 1768

William Orton, baptised 25 August 1757, son of Samuel O., admitted from St. Thomas Southwark; 3 January 1772 to Samuel Bale, Mr. of the *Mermaid* bound for Carolina.

William Carvel, baptised 12 May 1761, son of William C., admitted from Fawsley, Northamptonshire; 7 December 1773 with the consent of his said father of Edgcote Banbury, Northamptonshire, to serve Richard Oliver Esq., alderman, in Antigua.

Samuel Wallace, born 8 September 1757, son of Thomas W., admitted from St. Martin Ludgate; 3 September 1772 to his mother Mary W. of Lime Street Square to serve Mr. Erving, merchant, in Boston, New England.

Luke Rose, baptised 7 October 1757, son of John R., stationer, admitted from St. Peter at the Arches, Lincoln, in the place of Benjamin Sellwood; 15 June 1772 to his uncle-in-law, Mr. Henry Cock, on behalf of his mother Mary K., to serve Samuel Ball, Mr. of the *Britannia* in the Carolina trade.

Admissions in February 1769

David Jordan, baptised 7 October 1757, son of William J., goldsmith, admitted from Sandwich, Kent; 4 November 1772 to William Coombes, Mr. of the *Union* bound for South Carolina.

Joseph Thomas Fry, baptised 3 June 1759, son of William F., admitted from St. Mary Rotherhithe, Surrey; 6 March 1775 to his mother Catherine F. to serve Moses Henry, Mr. of the *Rachel* bound for Grenada.

Robert Davis, baptised 22 June 1760, son of Robert D., admitted from St. Clement Danes; 4 December 1776 to David Young, Mr.

of the *William & Elizabeth* bound for Antigua.

Thomas Rennoldson, baptised 8 February 1761, son of Thomas R., cordwainer, admitted from St. Olave Silver Street; 17 December 1777 to John Young, Mr. of the *Matthew* bound for St. Kitts.

John Spencer Padmore, baptised 13 June 1759, son of William P., admitted from New Brentford, Middlesex; 11 January 1774 to his uncle John Spencer. of New Brentford and Mr. John Mills of Great St. Helen's, merchant, to serve John Gardiner of St. Christopher's, barrister at law.

Sy Smith, baptised 6 October 1761, son of Thomas S., admitted from Bartlow, Cambridgeshire; 7 December 1776 to James Young, Mr. of the *Loyal Briton* bound for St. Kitts.

Charles Fowler, baptised 16 July 1757, son of Joseph F., admitted from Goltho, Lincolnshire, in the place of William Budge; 17 December 1776 to James Young, Mr. of the *Loyal Briton* bound for St. Kitts. [*William Budge was expelled because he was entered under the false name of Birch in order to evade the rule against having two brothers in the Hospital at the same time*].

Admissions in March 1770

Richard Baron, baptised 16 March 1759, son of Richard B., admitted from Bromley, Kent; 20 December 1775 to Thomas Oliver, Mr. of the *Pemberton* bound for St. Kitts.

John Vint, baptised 20 December 1761, son of John V., wheelwright, admitted from All Hallows Barking; 12 October 1776 to Benjamin Graham Esq. of London, merchant, to serve John Lindsey Esq. of Antigua, planter.

George Colley, baptised 8 December 1758, son of Richard C., admitted from All Hallows Staining; 14 January 1777 to his said father to serve Patrick Burke Esq. of St. Christopher's, merchant.

William Plant, baptised 16 November 1760, son of Samuel P., admitted from St. Dunstan in the West; 27 March 1775 to his said father to serve Mr. John Antill of New York, counsellor at law.

Admissions in February 1771

John Hollinworth, baptised 27 January 1764, son of John H., admitted from St. Dunstan Stepney; 22 December 1777 to Effingham Lawrence, Mr. of the *Edward* bound for New York.

George Stehn Stanford, baptised 20 August 1760, son of John S., admitted from Lingfield, Surrey; 1 February 1776 at the request of the mother Elizabeth S. of Woburn, Bedfordshire, to serve John Ranken Esq. of Jamaica, planter.

Michael Nightingale, baptised 31 July 1763, son of Michael N., admitted from St. Andrew Holborn; 27 January 1778 at the request of his aunt Elizabeth N. of Eltham, [Kent], to Mr. Joseph Stanfield, ironmonger of Foster Lane, to serve Mr. John Goosman of Kingston, Jamaica, merchant.

Thomas Gant, baptised 24 November 1761, son of Robert G., admitted from St. John Hackney; 25 April 1776 to his friend George Sanderson on behalf of his mother Elizabeth G. of Kingsland, [Middlesex], to serve William Abbott, Mr. of the *Canadian* bound for Quebec.

Robert Humbers, baptised 18 December 1763, son of James H., admitted from St. Giles in the Fields; 18 December 1779 to Jonathan Fryer, Mr. of the *Prince George* bound for Jamaica.

Admissions in March 1772

John Kemp, baptised 16 November 1763, son of John K., admitted from Benson, Oxfordshire; 1 February 1778 to his cousin Mr. Joseph Besouth on behalf of the mother Susan K., to serve Charles Winston Esq., Solicitor-General of Dominica.

John Thomas Henry Whitaker, baptised 8 May 1763, son of Rev. William W., admitted from Barton-under-Needwood, Staffordshire; 7 February 1778 with the consent of his said father to serve Charles Winston, Solicitor-General of Dominica.

Index of Names

References in bold print are to enrolled students. An asterisk indicates that there is more than one reference on the page.

142

Crockett (contd.)
    Thomas 15
Crockford, Luke 22
    Nathaniell **22**
    Rebecca 22
Crofts, Sarah 65
Croker, Robert **87**
    Thomas 87
Crompton, Anne 25
    Richard **25**
Crook, David **122**
    Jonathan 122*
Crookenden, Richard
    64
Crouch, Charles **107**
    Edward 116,**130**
    Isaac William **116**
    John 107
    Joseph 130
    Thomas **41**
Crow, Molford 30
Crowforth, Thomas 28
Crowley, Levinia 62
    Richard **62**
    William 62
Crump, Jane 47
    Nathaniel 66
Crumpler, John Galwith
    85
    Samuel 85
Cue, John **61**
Cull, Thomas 63
Cumming, Archabel 51
Cunningham, John 38
    Nathaniel 58
    William 74,82
Curling, Daniel 114
    George 114,116
    Robert 133
Currie, David 78,82,88,
    93
Curtis, Alexander 109
    Mary 19
    Robert 19
Cushee, John **36**
Cussack, Patrick 90
Cust, Peregrine 126

Dalby, Francis 123
Daling, William 124,
    127

Dallow, William **88**
Daniel, Charles **41**
    Samuel **64**
Dansie, Thomas 40
Darrack, Archibald 113
Davenport, John 104
    Robert **104**
Davers, Thomas 63
Davie, John 61
Davi(e)s, Ann 124
    Benjamin 118
    Elizabeth 55
    Hesketh 126
    James 108
    John **15,46**
    Nicholas 16
    Richard **124**
    Robert **135**
    Thomas **55,90**,124
    William **16**,37,46,**108**
Davison, John 74
Davy, Edward **56**
    Millicent 56
Dawes, Charles 98,101,
    113
    John **104**
Dawkins, Fearand 63
    Henry 72,104,117,
    118*,129
    James 92,115
Day, John **102**
    Lydia 102
    Richard 44
Deane, Richard **32**
Defell, John 128
Delamotte, John 51
    Peter 65
    Phillip **51**
Delap, Francis 59,77
Dellance, Oliver 96
Delves, Hugh 114
    John **114**
Dennis, Frances 50
    George **50**
    John 50
Denston, John **82**
    William 82
Denton, John **62**
    Richard 62
Dibon, William **120**
Dickary, Peter 22
Dickenson, James 54

Dickinson, George **34**
    Margaret 37
    William 37,130
Diggs, Cole 51
Dingley, Charles 120
Dixon, Charles **117**
Dobbins, Sarah 36
Dodd, George 31
    Michael 34,91
    William **31**
Dodsworth, Charles 78
Dolbeare, Benjamin 87
Dolby, William **21**
Dongworth, John **126**
    William 126
Dorrell, William 105
Dotin, Thomas 73,75
Dottin, William 131
Doughty, Charles **115**
Douglas(s), James 62,63*
    James George 91
    John 91
Dove, Thomas **70**
Downe, John 43
Dracott, Richard 54,**77**
    Timothy 77
    William **54**
Drake, Edmond 21
    George 126,129
    Richard 70
    Roger 70,72,76,77*,84
Drakeford, Richard 121
Draycott, John **25**
    Mary 25
Drinkwater, Edmond
    112
    John **112**
    Mary 113
Driver, Robert **38**
Droste, John **110**
Duer, John 71
Dumbleton, Abraham
    12
Dummer, Phillip 73
Dunbar, Charles 85
    George 85,93
    John 100
    Mary 41
    Willard 100
    William 94,96,100
Dunbrack, George **96**
    Thomas 96

Trippett *alias* Triplett,
    Thomas **15**
    William 15
Trott, Nicholas 46
Trueman, Thomas 43,
    51,53,54,72,88,106
Tryon, Thomas 45,58*,
    69,70,73,75,83,88,
    95,96,99,103
    William 45,55,73
Tucker, Robert 39
Tuffe, John 113
    William **113**
Tuffery, Daniel Phillip
    58
    John 58
    Mary 58
Tullideph, Walter 94,
    96,104
Turner, Elizabeth 75
    Jeremia 37
    Jonathan **75**
    Joseph 56
    Mary 81
    Samuel 98,122
Tweedy, James 69
    Timothy **69**
Tyer, Elizabeth 85
    Henry 85
    Richard **85**
Tyzack, Edward 53,90

Underhill, Joane 24
    Sarah 21
Underwood, Joane 46
    John 46
    Thomas **46**
Unet, George **102**
    Richard 102
    Sarah 102
Upholfens, John 49
    Peter **49**

Vaile, William **20**
Vallotton, Francis
    Edward 129
Vanhorne, Philip 91
Vassall, Florentius 77,
    78,82,88,93
Vaughan, James **16**

Vaughan (contd.)
    Roger 16
Venable, Hannah 35
    James **35**
    John 35
Venables, Catherine
    109
Venn, Stephen 115
Venny, John 115
Verchild, Jasper 69
Vernon, Francis 73
    John 83
    Margaret 73
    Thomas **73**
Verstille, Peter **101**
    William 101
Vesey, Joseph 111
Vicars, Thomas **12**
Vickery, Elinor 44
Vincent, Dickinson **74**
    Frederick **28**
    John 28
    Richard 74
Vinicombe, John **113**
    Mary 113
Vining, Abraham 52
Vint, John **136**

Wade, John 102
    Samuel 107
Wadeson, Samuel 58
Wadham, John **106**
Wager, Elizabeth 110
Waite, John 75
Walcott, Eyare 56
Waldy, James 32
Walford, John **89**
    Tompson 89
Walker, Abraham **73**
    Alexander 92,93
    Anthony 47,110
    George 42,59,73
    James 34,50,**101**
    Job 103
    John **103**
    Mary 73
    Peacock 47
    Thomas 79,101,129,
    131
Walklate, Sarah 130
Wall, Tobias 59,74,78

Wallace, Mary 135
    Samuel **135**
    Thomas 135
Wallband, Mary 47
Wallcott, William 98
Walley, Samuel 64
Wallington, Benjamin
    21
    William 21
Wallis, Edward 17
    Humphrey **84**
    John 84
    Joseph **17**
Walmsley, Edward 87
    Sarah 93
    Thomas 69
    William **69**
Walnar, John **101**
    William 101
Walrond, Main Swete
    133
Walsh, Delacourt 129,
    131
Walter, James Siddall
    133
Walters, Ellinor 23
    James **23**
    John 23
Walton, Isaac 107
Wane, George 93
Ward, Isaac **15**
    Jacob **15,44**
    Martha 82
    Richard 15*
    Thomas **82**
    Ursula 44
    William **134**
Warner, Ashton 73,95,
    103
    Daniel 106,114
    Thomas 98,106
Warren, Dominick 106
    Elizabeth 106
    John 95
    Josiah **106**
    Miles 106
    Thomas 17,95
Warter, Francis 57
Washington, George 7
Waterman, Lawrence
    64
    Priscilla 64

Index of Names

Index of Ships

Index of Ships